CW01086186

SELL

IT!

How to Sell Your Business and Enjoy a Richer, Happier Future

Christine Nicholson

First published in 2021 in the UK
3P Publishing, C E C, London Road,
Corby, NN17 5EU
A catalogue number for this book is available from
the British Library

ISBN: 978-1-913740-41-2

Cover: James Mossop

Dedication:

Gladys Banks

Lt Dick Tough RN

(Both sadly no longer with us in the flesh but still making a difference because they were here)

Colin Potter

Tim Maclure

(Still adding to a positive planet to live on and making a difference)

All "superhero" mentors who had huge impact on my life.

I wouldn't be where I am without their guidance

CONTENTS

INTRODUCTION..1

THE DREAM.. 1

THE REALITY 2

WHO IS THIS BOOK FOR?... 5

WHY AM I WRITING ABOUT THIS?... 7

WHY NOW?.. 13

TIMING IS EVERYTHING 13

PART 1 17

SUCCESSFUL SELLING 19

BUSINESS SALES – SUCCESS FACTORS 19

SELLING FAILURE.. 23

BUSINESS VALUE 31

WHAT AFFECTS YOUR BUSINESS VALUE?................................... 31

WHY ARE DIFFERENT VALUATION METHODS ARE USED? 34

WHAT STOPS A BUSINESS BEING SOLD?..................................... 36

GET YOUR BUSINESS VALUED 38

THE SELL IT MODEL 41

OVERVIEW 41

WHAT IS THE S.E.L.L. I.T. MODEL? 42

WHY S.E.L.L. I.T.? 45

PART 2 47

SUCCESSION PLANNING 49

WHY DO YOU NEED A SUCCESSION PLAN?.................................. 49

WHO IS THE NEXT LEADER?... 53

BUILDING A TEAM 58

EXIT READY **63**

WHAT IS EXIT READINESS? 63

UNDERSTANDING THE ESSENTIALS 66

BEING P.E.R.F.E.C.T. 69

EXPLORE THE OPTIONS 79

UNDERSTAND THE JOURNEY 81

LETTING GO **85**

WHY IS LETTING GO A CHALLENGE? 85

THE 3 ROLES OF A BUSINESS OWNER 89

OWNERSHIP MINDSET AND OWNERSHIP THINKING 96

PREPARING FOR WHAT'S NEXT 98

LEGALS **101**

GETTING THE RIGHT LAWYER 101

THE LEGAL DOCUMENTS 103

WHAT TO PREPARE FOR 107

UNDERSTAND THAT SELLING A BUSINESS IS DIFFICULT ... 109

NEGOTIATING FACTORS 112

INFORMATION MEMORANDUM **117**

WHAT IS IT? 117

FINDING A BUYER 121

THE TRANSACTION **131**

THE COMPONENTS 131

THE FINAL NEGOTIATIONS 140

POPPING THE CHAMPAGNE CORKS 144

PART 3 .... **147**

GETTING STARTED **149**

FINDING THE ADVISORS 149

Start with Strategic Planning 155

KNOW YOUR BUSINESS **163**

Valuation 163

Benchmarking 167

Non-Financial Risks 174

Exit Readiness 178

Credit worthiness 180

ACTION PLAN **181**

What Gets Measured.... 181

Where to Start 183

Reverse Due Diligence 186

Employee Participation 187

The Final Event 190

WHAT NEXT? **193**

What are you going to do now? 193

The checklists 195

NEED HELP? **207**

ABOUT THE AUTHOR – WHO AM I? **213**

REFERENCES & READING **219**

Introduction

The Dream

After years of building your business from scratch to a sizable asset, probably your biggest financial asset, you wake up tomorrow and decide it's time to sell. You look forward and envisage that in 6 months you will be taking your long-suffering family on that holiday of a lifetime, having sold your business for several million pounds. You've handed over the keys and never looked back.

In this fairy tale scenario, the business model is perfect with high margins and steady overheads. Consistent positive cash flow allows you to invest in the on-going growth and development of the business, your employees and yourself.

You are focused on strategy and supporting the leadership. Your team are focused on delivery and know exactly what they need to do, when they need to do it AND, most importantly, are empowered to get on with it. Truth is the business doesn't really need you at all.

You're there because you've the passion to drive the business onwards to greater success. Every day is a new opportunity to serve your customers to enable them to have a better life. You'd still do it even if you were not being paid.

Do you recognise your business in this story?

The Reality

Building a business is hard. It's demanding on a physical, emotional, and financial level. The stories that get into the press and magazines are of the successes, glossing over the tough road travelled to get there.

At the beginning it's all hands to the pump just getting off the ground. Small victories are celebrated, like your first customer signing up and the first payment going into the bank. Then the day to day of running a business takes over and the frantic stage of the business is in full flow. Well intentioned thoughts of getting paperwork in order are put to one side for a day when you have the time to think about it. You've thought about the shareholder agreement but, as you are all getting on, what's the rush?

2

As you get a bit bigger and need staff, you take on your first employees. You find people who can do lots of things effectively in a small business. This includes a "capability jane" who manages to keep a lot of plates spinning and never letting one drop. The first members of your team work in parallel with you, deferring all decision making to you. They know what to do for the most part but anything outside of the normal is handled by you.

As you get more customers, you get more staff and more issues. Every day there is a fire to put out, a query to answer or a problem to solve. Not every customer is getting the same experience. It becomes a bit hit and miss depending on who is handling each customer or prospect. There is a golden thread of your company culture running through the business, but it isn't consistent.

Years go by. You are in the daily cycle of reacting, which means you aren't leading. Your energy and passion dips because you aren't doing what you hoped you would be. Some days you dread going into the business because you don't know what you are going to deal with. All your plans at the beginning of the year, that didn't get written down but are in your head, are not getting done.

No one else knows what the long-term plans are so only you can direct the business.

You are tired. Selling becomes attractive, especially when you hear from one of your business owning friends of his business sale.

He's now millions the richer and free to get on with the next phase of his life. He's got ideas of exciting new business opportunities that he can invest in while still looking after his family, private schools for the children and holidays to exotic places. If he can do it, maybe it's time you did too?

You've an idea of a number that you think your business is worth. It's a big number and it feels good because it represents the years of sacrifice you've made. The long hours, not being paid in the early days, struggling to get new customers and keep existing ones. Coping with the various dramas of employing people – sometimes the wrong people, who take ages to get rid of. It's compensation for the missed family time, nativity plays, sports days, and parent evenings. It's a reward to your spouse who's made sure everything in your home life has been covered in your absence and been patient on the holidays where you've been glued to your phone.

But do you really know how much your business is worth to someone else?

The truth is no one cares about any of those things when they are looking at buying your business. They care about return on investment. They want a business that has as little risk as possible, that generates net positive cash flow and is full of people who know what to do in their designated roles. They are looking for certainty, consistency, and clarity. They measure this against their own risk appetite and the criteria they set for their investment plans.

In short, they are interested in how this business is going to serve _their_ needs.

The better shape your business is in, the easier it is to find a buyer AND complete the sale process. Selling a business is about more than just the profitability – that's just the start!

Who is this book for?

If you recognise yourself in either of the two scenarios, then you are in the right place!

For motivated business founders, the route to exit is often seen as limited to selling to another company, trying to handover to the next generation or simply closing the doors having bled

5

enough money out of it while it is still running. There are so many more options, and each option is not mutually exclusive to others.

The harsh reality for many of business owners is they either:

- Stay in the weeds of daily operations and never get to plan what needs to happen to allow them to sell – leaving them with fewer choices (sometimes no choice at all)

- Tell themselves "I am never leaving this business" – which is sticking their head in the sand because 100% of business owners DO leave their businesses; no one is immortal

or

- Hope for an offer to randomly land and then let the buyer take the lead because they don't know what the process is and how to prepare fully. Often giving away a lot of value that they could have kept for themselves.

Too many great businesses are floundering in mediocrity through a lack of knowledge as to what makes a great business. Too many business owners reduce the value of their business by working long hours and keeping their business reliant on themselves.

Significant value and potential is being lost to the UK economy because of poor business transfers between one generation and the next.

Why am I writing about this?

The one thing I understand is the problems that businesses and their founders experience when they are trying to get the value from their lifetime of work.

Having built my own companies from scratch and come to the rescue of businesses that are on their knees (the owners are usually literally on them and desperate to extract the value they've put in!), I know what it takes to get from unsaleable to exit success AND how businesses get exit ready in the first place.

If you want to benefit from the value locked in your business, the best thing to do is to start thinking about what it is YOU as the owner want out of your business. If you are just starting out, beginning with the end in mind is a great place to start. It is much easier, cheaper, and quicker to plan successful exit options from the start.

If you are already a significant way along your business journey, now is a good time to take a deep breath and think about what needs to happen for you and your family to benefit from all the value you've built.

Now is always a good time to think about "what next?" and "what if?" No one knows what's going to happen tomorrow but being prepared for the most common likelihoods means the assets you've been building over your lifetime are protected, and your family are looked after. It just takes a bit of planning and preparation.

That said it is not easy, it is still hard work

When I started writing this book, I kept in mind an old colleague from 20+ years ago who set me off on my mission to improve businesses. To protect the privacy of his family, let's call him Trevor (he is a real person).

Trevor had left school at 17 because he'd got his girlfriend pregnant and "did the right thing" and married her (it was the early 70s). He struggled through a couple of jobs before realizing that he could set up on his own. He started building a product in his garage when he was 24.

8

By the time he was 35, his business had moved into new premises and Trevor was employing 20 people. He'd also brought in a business partner to get the business growing and take the pressure off himself as being the only decision maker.

Life was pretty good, he now had 3 children, a bigger house, and more outgoings. Roll forward another decade and Trevor met the love of his life – and decided to make a massive life change. He left his wife and started divorce proceedings. He bought a new house, solely in his own name. He started preparing to marry his new lady. It all looked like a bright new future in a new life. And he started to think about how he could spend less time at work in the business.

Trevor did not have a will. Or a shareholder agreement with his business partner. In fact, they'd been so busy building the business that they hadn't really thought about how they would protect the value they were building. They were both heads down, getting on with keeping the wheels turning of what was now a £10m turnover enterprise.

Trevor was still a big part of the business and managed ALL the customer relationships. His business partner was the back-office guy and kept the wheels of the operation in motion. He was also a minority shareholder and had limited voting rights but that was ok because of the verbal agreement that he had with Trevor about the future of the business.

While Trevor was making the new house ready for his new wife, and he was still legally married to his first wife, he fell off a ladder. This triggered a devastating chain of events. Sadly, Trevor died.

With no will, his estate transferred to his not-quite-ex-wife, including the house he bought with the intention of living with his new lady. His embittered wife decided she wanted to become involved in the business despite knowing nothing about it. The shareholding transferred to her and gave her voting rights and the right to appoint directors.

With no clear instruction this allowed her to start spending company funds on all sorts of activities that didn't add value to the business. She decided to take over sales and marketing. She crushed the spirit of the team and they started to leave. It was a disaster. Within 2 years the business was closed, and a significant amount of the value lost – as well as nearly 100 jobs.

How do you increase your opportunities for successfully protecting and extracting the value of your business?

This book shows you a tried and tested framework – S.E.L.L.I.T. – showing you options and "what needs to happen" so that you can do the right things in your business to get a richer, happier future. Often, it's doing less that allows both you and your business to thrive.

Each stage of the process allows you to plan, review and decide on actions that have a direct impact on the value of your business without wasting precious time and cash. You'll learn how to add value and enjoy the process and get more value along the way.

Life is hard enough without having the extra pressure of learning how to sell a business effectively when you don't have the experience or knowledge – or the time to learn.

This book takes the pressure off by showing you what you need to pay attention to BEFORE you must leave your business! It is much better to be prepared and be proactive than reacting to circumstances. You'll be less stressed, more productive and a much better leader of your business as a result – and your family and friends will thank you for it too!

Why Now?

"Better 3 hours too soon than 3 minutes too late."
William Shakespeare

Timing is Everything

Being prepared means you are in a stronger position to take advantage of whatever opportunities arise. There are now more businesses than ever before. More people are taking control of their own futures and starting out on their own.

Is the dream of building something bigger than a job driving you to take more risks? Are you creating a business that has long lasting value?

The sacrifices that founders make are justified by the potential rewards when the business is eventually sold. With future value in mind, do you think of your business as your pension fund? Are you mentally, physically, and financially investing in your business for your retirement?

You are not alone. As a result, there are more businesses than ever before with owners thinking about retirement and looking for "exit" options. When a business becomes your pension fund, it's even more important to know how to extract the value from your business.

But there is a horrifying statistic that many business owners turn a blind eye to:

80% of businesses that are attempting to sell do not get sold.

Most business owners only ever sell one business. They are personally poorly prepared (or not at all). Neither is their business. Preparation for a sale starts with understanding the process and the position of the buyer. Knowing what the buyer is looking for and how it affects the value of the business means the seller gets on the front foot and ready for the final negotiation and ultimately the contract for the sale.

This book shows you the journey you need to go on to sell a business and how to be prepared so that you get the most from a lifetime of work. The added benefits of being ready for a transaction well before the transfer of ownership is you have a business that is easier to operate, more enjoyable and less stressful for everyone, including yourself.

Your business will also be worth more!

If you've never sold a business before and don't know what to expect, then you are definitely in the right place. The same goes for buying a business, it's the same process in reverse. It's time consuming, stressful, and challenging. It's an adventure.

Some questions you need to ask yourself before launching on this journey are:

1. Why am I selling?
    Knowing and having clarity on your reasons helps you and your advisors position your business for the right buyer.

2. Is it the right time?
    Having a finger on the pulse of the market can help you sell for the best value and being ready means you can respond to market changes.

3. Am I ready?
    It's a good idea to get the business in good shape but that's only part of it. Are you personally ready to let go of the business?

4. Is the business in the best shape to sell?
    A bit like a house in good repair sells more easily and for a better price than one that isn't, it's the same in the business world. Being in good shape makes due diligence easier.

5. What's it worth?

   Having a realistic idea of your business value means you're prepared for offers, especially if they are unsolicited. Knowing your business value means you are less likely to leave money on the table.

6. Who are the buyers?

   It's likely you already know of potential buyers, even if you haven't given it a lot of thought. The right broker can find the ideal buyer for you, discreetly, if you haven't got an offer in play. Finding the right buyer for you and your business is something you should give thought to when exploring your reasons for selling. You have more options than you might think.

In the same way a sensible person wouldn't choose to climb a mountain without some preparation, selling or buying a business is a much better experience if you have the right "kit". You need to make sure you don't take your eye off the business while you are going through the process. Just because a sale process starts is no guarantee it will end with a successful transaction.

"If your presence doesn't add value, your absence won't make a difference."
Zero Dean

PART 1

Successful Selling

Business sales – success factors

Even when the world seems to be heading for economic meltdown with financial crashes, global pandemics and stock market bubbles bursting, businesses still get sold and buyers still buy.

Where a business shows it can give a return to its investors, there will always be buying and selling activity. Most data available in the public domain relates to larger transactions and, whilst it is harder to sell a smaller, privately held business, it still happens on a daily basis. The principal factors are timing and readiness for both parties.

In the UK there is a significant amount of inward investment by overseas buyers. In the last 3 calendar months of 2020 this amounted to over £4.3 billion alone. The buyer for your business may not be a UK based company or investor. Cross border acquisitions have been increasing. Domestic (UK-UK) activity has been decreasing and halving to £2.2 billion in the last 3 months of 2020. Equally if you are a UK buyer, it is now more likely that you are looking at overseas acquisitions, evidenced by the £4.5 billion of outward M&A activity in the last quarter of 2020. (ONS Statistical Bulletin March 2021)

After much delay in some buying and selling activity in 2020, there is a lot of capital available from investors. Estimates indicate that buyers are sitting on trillions of investment funds.

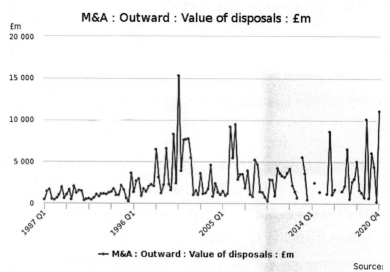

M&A : Outward : Value of disposals : £m

→ M&A : Outward : Value of disposals : £m

Source:

Source: ONS Statistical Bulletin, March 2021

Confidence in the market is increasing as the signs of post-pandemic recovery come to the fore with vaccines etc. This leads to an increase in buying activity. Some of this is going to be in the "distressed assets" as businesses face the fall out of economic impact of government interventions being removed such as furlough.

Buyers are likely to pay a great deal of attention to the business fundamentals, not just the financials. Successful sales can be made easier by getting your business "exit ready". The longer you show that your business has been in this state of readiness, the more comfort you are giving to the buyer. The acquiring investors see that you aren't in a rush to off load the business but have been preparing for when you want to leave and when the timing is right for you, your business and the other stakeholders.

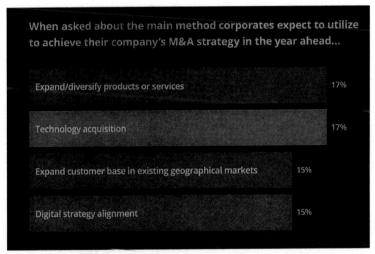

Source: PWC Global Trends Report, 2020

Malcolm Lloyd, Global Deals Leader, Partner, PwC Spain points out in the PWC Global Trends Report "With so much capital out there, good businesses are commanding high multiples... and achieving them. If this continues - and I believe it will - then the need to double down on value creation is now more relevant than ever for successful M&A." Equally Deloitte's US M&A Trend Report 2020 identified that investors are likely to keep on acquiring companies and pay more for them.

Strategy drivers for these investors are the need to fill gaps in portfolios, especially capability in technology, digital strategy, and geographic spread of customers.

In some industries the competition for acquisitions drives value higher, especially in those industries that support digital and enabling technology-based assets. In these cases, the non-financial aspects of your business come in for much closer inspection. Those who prepare and implement good practices become the winners. Some business sectors are going to find it more of a struggle to maintain previously buoyant valuations as their business models have shown higher levels of risk associated with business disruption. Those that adapt to the new digital age win, those who don't, lose.

Acquirers as well as sellers who are clear on their strategy for transfer of ownership are better placed to succeed and create future value from transactions more easily. One of the keys to successful acquisition is a robust due diligence process. This includes detailed analysis of commercial, operational, and financial variables. Value is attributed to non-financial aspects of the business such as resilience and how future value can be added after the acquisition. Sellers who show a route to added value are more attractive and easier to sell.

22

Selling Failure

80% of all businesses that are for sale never get sold. And the main reason is that most business owners do not have the knowledge or experience of the sale process.

A lack of appropriate information means they are poorly prepared (i.e., not at all) and fall at one of the many stumbling blocks that they experience along the way. Most business owners only go through the sale process once. It's often a very painful experience. It is emotionally draining and mentally demanding. The sale process distracts you from the day to day running of your business, which hits you hard if you are heavily involved in operations.

Getting though the sale process is just the first step. If you are involved in an earn-out or deferred consideration deal you need to think about what future success looks like. Many "mergers" do not add up to greater value.

Failure can happen at two key points in the process. Failure to get the deal across the line in the first place. And failure to create value and get the expected return from the deal after the acquisition. Let's look briefly at both.

Failure pre-acquisitions - getting across the line

As you'll read over and over again in this book, most business owners only sell one business – their own.

There are 7 big mistakes inexperienced sellers make:

1. Taking their eye off the business during the process

2. Not getting the right advisors involved early enough

3. Not getting a professional valuation before going to sell

4. Not being prepared enough for the sale process

5. Only finding one buyer (or accepting an unsolicited offer at face value)

6. Not being fully committed to selling

7. Not having a post-exit plan (for themselves or their business)

There are some factors that guarantee failure on the sale process:

- Owner involvement (or lack of)

- Valuation

- Mis-aligned expectations

When an owner is not fully engaged and involved in the sale process, it has a higher chance of failing at various stages. It's important to make sure you are connected to the process and do not delegate it all to your exit team.

Unrealistic valuation expectations often mean the business is not able to be sold. For it's true value. The value is what someone else will pay for it, not what effort you feel you have put into it.

In the early stages of the process it's important to be clear and honest about your expectations. It's better to find out that the buyer is not ideal as early as possible. Being honest with yourself about what you will and will not accept can be a challenge if you really want to sell your business in a short time frame.

Getting the right help at the various stages is key to achieving a successful sale BUT, and it's a big but, you need to be involved. Selling your business is not a job to completely delegate to the advisors. There are times when you wonder why you are paying advisors because you are being bombarded with questions and demands for information.

Ducking out of the process is not an option and it is made a lot easier if you are prepared. It is also a lot less stressful and has a higher degree of success.

Leaving it to the advisors leaves a lot of capacity for key elements of the business to be left to interpretation. What might be common practice to advisors might not be what the seller is expecting and may even be a deal breaker at the 11th hour. More owner involvement and engagement saves time and money.

When a valuation is based on just numbers, it can often lead to an initial offer in excess of the final negotiated price. The value of your business is about far more than just the numbers that are presented in your statutory accounts and your forecasts. Undertaking a pre-due diligence assessment allows you to look at your business through the same lens as a potential acquirer and address the weaknesses inherent in the current structure of the business. This is likely to avoid price chipping or post-acquisition claw backs or claims.

Often an acquirer is a larger organisation, and they look at expansion as a way of creating value and getting a higher return on their investment. Are you already working at capacity and cannot grow as fast as the new owner expected? This causes a misalignment of expectations.

If you are tied into an earnout or deferred consideration based on future performance this is going to cause frustration. It's the same when integration costs start piling up because there was a poor understanding of the way the two parties work or due to major cultural differences.

The sale process has a lot of moving parts. Changes in the environment can bring a deal to its knees for reasons outside the buyer and seller's control. The global financial crisis and the global pandemic are cases in point. More than 50% of sales activity never completes. It's worth knowing at each stage when to proceed or stop rather than keep going on in the hope that something improves in the process.

Don't rely on the sale process completing just because it started – have a Plan B if it falls through. Most importantly know what you want out of it and know when you are at the point you want to walk away. This helps you make the right decision for you earlier in the process.

Failure post-acquisitions - culture, systems, capacity

According to a 2016 Harvard Business Review article, (Lewis and McKone, 2016) the failure rate for mergers and acquisitions (M&A) to add value is higher than 60%. There's evidence that is a trend that continues today.

When two companies come together, it can be like planets colliding. Bringing different cultures, personalities and operating practices together is often a challenge that isn't considered by either party during the sale and purchase phase. At a basic level often the first hurdle is different IT systems.

One example of this was a previous "services" focused client who was acquired by a much larger global "product" focused company. Different cultures aside, when it came to merging their email systems chaos ensued and resulted in most of the UK staff moving from a single email address to 3 and in some cases 4 addresses.

Sometimes it's the simplest of things that causes the most problems.

What's required is a clear post-acquisition integration strategy. This is often either completely ignored or only implemented as lip service. The more transparent and realistic the process is, involving as many stakeholders as possible, the more chance there is of adding value.

In the BCG 2020 M&A Report, their survey into alternative deals (i.e. not 100% takeovers) showed many acquirers didn't have a clear post-acquisition roadmap for creating value or experienced poor governance after the deal.

They list success factors such as early preparation, robust due diligence and clearly defined post-acquisition governance. Being aware of cultural differences (and similarities) and addressing integration issues are often missed in a traditional approach to deals. They are key factors in M&A activity that contribute to avoidance of failure yet are often seldom seen in smaller and privately owned business transactions.

In the Deloitte M&A Trends report, they surveyed reasons for M&A failure to generate the potential value out of a deal, post-acquisition. It's clear that internal factors far outweigh the number of external factors. The biggest risks come from within.

Source: Deloitte M&A Trends report, 2020

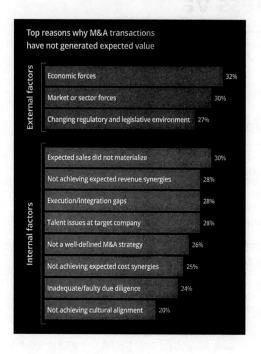

Top reasons why M&A transactions
have not generated expected value

External factors

Economic forces	32%
Market or sector forces	30%
Changing regulatory and legislative environment	27%

Internal factors

Expected sales did not materialize	30%
Not achieving expected revenue synergies	28%
Execution/integration gaps	28%
Talent issues at target company	28%
Not a well-defined M&A strategy	26%
Not achieving expected cost synergies	25%
Inadequate/faulty due diligence	24%
Not achieving cultural alignment	20%

Business Value

"No one is more hated than he who speaks the truth."

Plato

What affects your business value?

When business owners think about the value of their business, they rarely do it objectively. Most business owners do not know how to value their business from the perspective of a buyer.

If they do know valuation methods, they often apply entirely subjective criteria so that the result gives them the number they are looking for. Thinking like a buyer means detaching all emotion from the way you think about your business – and usually that means getting someone else to look at the value. Even then it's hard not to "shoot the messenger" when the results come through and it's not the news you are looking for.

Getting an objective valuation for your business from someone who looks at all the risk factors in your business is something any business owner should do as early as possible. And keep doing it on a regular basis to see how you are improving.

The value of your business is about more than just the numbers.

31

The four most important risk factors a buyer looks at in the first instance are:

- Over reliance on the business owner

- Concentration of revenue on a small number of customers

- Lack of financial reporting (or poor-quality financial information);

- The rhythm of revenue generation (recurring revenue)

Looking at these issues objectively, they make sense not just to a buyer but to a business owner. If the business can't run without you, then you can never take a relaxing holiday or prolonged absence. What happens if you become ill or incapacitated? Or worse? If the entire customer base relies on the relationship the clients have with the business owner this poses a significant risk to the immediate and long-term revenue of the business. This is what a buyer is acquiring and investing in.

Without historic financial reporting the buyer finds it hard to see the real operational performance of the business. The robustness of the business financial reports give comfort to the buyers who are investing in a return on their investment. It's easier to sell if you help the buyer see the value and not make him work for it. The harder a buyer must work to understand the numbers, the more nervous they get and the more risk they see.

One way of looking at your business is asking the question "Would I buy this for the amount of money I'm asking?" and secondly "Where would I get a return on the investment I'm making?" This is the first step into the buyer's shoes.

The more risk the buyer sees in the business, the lower value they place on the investment – or they walk away before wasting more money on the due diligence process. Due diligence costs both parties in time, energy, and money. For the unprepared seller it also adds greater levels of anxiety and stress, especially if there is time pressure to sell because of circumstances.

The great advantage of addressing these 4 factors, whether you are planning to sell now or in the future, is that you are adding value to your business as you work through them. By removing the reliance of the business from being entirely on your shoulders, you'll also find you have more time and better performance from your team. Win-Win!

Why are different valuation methods used?

There are many ways to value a business and each one has its benefits and weaknesses. Knowing which one is best for you puts you ahead of the competition

The most common methods used in professional M&A firms (including banking, private equity etc.) are:

- EBITDA (earnings) multiple

- Revenue multiple

- Discounted Cash Flow

- Precedent Transactions (consensus price based on other similar transactions)

A business with recurring revenues and high customer loyalty has a higher future value than one that has one-off purchases and must constantly source new customers, even if they both have the same EBITDA for the last 3 years. Thus, different valuation methods are used.

Understanding how your business is valued by potential buyers gives you a head start in the sale process because you can prepare your business accordingly. Valuing your business using a different valuation method to your buyers sets you on the wrong path, with unrealistic expectations. Knowing what buyers in your industry look for means you have insights that put you ahead of other sellers. Or it may even get you looking outside your industry and into other sectors for a buyer who is looking for a break into your industry sector or who operates in a complementary space.

I'm not going to go into the details of valuation methods here. That's worthy of an entire book.

The truth is you shouldn't have to worry about every aspect of the process. You've been busy building your business, not learning to become an M&A (mergers and acquisitions), legal and corporate finance specialist. Here I just want to eliminate some uncertainty and make sure you have the tools and knowledge to enable your business to thrive into the future.

What stops a business being sold?

When a buyer starts looking at purchasing your business, they assess every aspect of your company to make sure it is optimised.

Your business is about more than just the numbers. Profit is important, but what are the other factors a buyer looks for in a business? The way your business operates is key to its value. Most businesses do not consciously address the culture and behaviour in the business, yet it has a big impact on a buyer's perception of the value. It shows up in how your team work together, what your processes are and how the customer experiences your products and services.

How your business has behaved in the past has a significant impact on the way a buyer views risks associated with the company. This includes its relationships with statutory bodies like HMRC i.e., paying taxes on time, submitting statutory returns etc.

If you are essential to your business and it can't operate without you, that poses a major risk for an acquirer. Your customer and supplier contracts are scrutinised as part of the due diligence process to ensure continuity of revenue after the completion.

It goes with the territory that your financials come under the microscope. Buyers look for order and regular management accounts as well as your annual compliance of statutory requirements.

The legal structure of your company may make the sale process more difficult. Getting this in order is good business. If your company owns property, you may wish to decide whether you want to include it in a future sale of the company or if you want to keep the property to generate rental income.

In my first complex exit, a family-owned business had growth through acquisition over a period of 50 years. Starting out in construction, they extended into shipping, logistics, importing fruit and ship building. It might have seemed a bit random, but each acquisition was a solution to a problem at the time. The way the business was collectively put together didn't make a lot of sense.

It's a bit like extending your house every year without planning permission or a plan for what it is going to be used for. The owners and directors spent 18 months getting the right legal structures in place to make it easier to sell to the right buyer. They knew exactly who the potential buyers were before they started the process.

Get your business valued

Business valuation, from a business-owners perspective, is an emotional subject. It's easy to Google the concept of valuing a business and often you can get a rough idea of your value using a basic industry standard formula.

Most of these relate to open market sales for listed companies where publicly available data is used. The reality is that these methods cannot give an accurate value in many cases for privately held companies.

In conversations with business owners looking to sell, I always ask "Do you know what it's worth today?" The most common answer is to a completely different question, which is "I'm not selling for less than £x million". With no idea what their business is worth in the market, it is common for owners (especially founders) to apply a rule of sacrifice value i.e., how much of myself, my time and sacrifice have I put into this business?

The bad news is buyers don't care about any of that. They only care about their return on investment and their attitude towards risk.

A professional valuation before you go to market is essential so that you can have a realistic idea of where bids are likely to come in. It helps you manage your expectations in the process. If you think your business is worth £20m but all the evidence points toward a £2m valuation, there is going to be a lot of wasted time and money trying to find a buyer that pays the expected price.

A valuation starts with your year-end numbers.
Those alone will not get your business sold.

With value expectation gaps you'd be better spending your time and effort getting help with how to grow it to match your financial needs. You can't decide when to sell unless you know the value of your business today. Equally you can't focus on the right value building activity if you don't know what impact it has.

When a buyer is valuing your company, they look at every aspect of your business including an assessment of:

- Business operations

- Financial reporting

- Your role in the business

- Customer concentration

- The team

- Risks inherent in your business and industry

- How you perform against your competitors

Hundreds of other criteria are reviewed depending on what they are looking to achieve in the acquisition of your entity.

"Visibility without value is vanity."
Bernard Kelvin Clive

The SELL IT Model

"Luck is not a business model."

Anthony Bourdain

Overview

The journey to selling or transferring ownership of your business has some common and critical elements. No matter what method of transition you have, these are all encompassed in the S.E.L.L.I.T. model.

For some business owners, the process may be shorter and simpler than others. Figuring out where you want to be is the first step towards getting there. Many business owners never think about the way they are going to leave their business even though there is a 100% certainty that they will leave one day – one way or another. As a business owner myself the exit plan was always in play, with contingency plans if anything unexpected happened to any of the key people in the business, including myself.

Having worked with or spoken to thousands of business owners over the last 3 decades, selling their business has been a consistent theme of conversation. Yet most are still in the dark as to the choices they have (selling isn't the only way to extract value) or the actual process that they need to prepare to go

41

through. Time to dispel the mystery and explore what really happens when you want to prepare to leave your business.

What is the S.E.L.L. I.T. model?

There are 6 key steps in the transfer of ownership of a business. Each one has its own challenges, plans and required actions. Each one also has different participants and requires specialist help. Knowing who to get involved at each stage helps keep your team focused on the outcomes for each stage whilst still aiming at the global goal:

- Succession Planning

- Exit Planning

- Letting Go

- Legal requirements

- Information Memorandum (Sale Documentation)

- Transaction

"There is no harm in hoping for the best as long as you have planned for the worst."
Stephen King

In describing the model, it's worth defining what each of the elements is before going into the detail of what each step requires in terms of actions. Clarity for you as the business owner means you'll be able to get the appropriate help and as the right questions to get a full understanding of what happens, when and who needs to be involved.

Succession Planning is an essential part of any business' strategic plan and their business continuity plan. Even if you are never going to sell your business, you will leave it one day, one way or another. So will everybody else in it. Having a succession plan is a key part of your business resilience and value. Succession planning is about the people, leadership and management of your business.

Exit Planning is about the ownership of the business. Whilst you might be tempted to think that the ownership structure of the business doesn't affect your employees, suppliers or customers, this would be a misconception for many businesses. Often the business owner is the relationship owner of the commercial connections in a business.

If the business owner leaves, so do customers, staff and suppliers. Exit planning mitigates that outcome as well as how and when a business owner transfers ownership and control of the business. This includes planning for the unexpected.

Letting Go is all about the business owner. When you have founded a company, built it over a period and are emotionally attached to it, letting go can be a challenge.

Legals are the contracts and other legally binding documents that you'll have to get on top of as you go through the sale process. Knowing what they include ahead of time means you're prepared and understand how all the pieces fit in place. Knowing the process and documents saves you lots of time and money.

Information Memorandum is your invitation to potential buyers and is a taster of what your business offers them in terms of potential investment.

The Transaction is the final sale which consists of the final negotiations, the contract paperwork and the transfer of funds. This is the culmination of all your hard work and the final hurdle to get across.

Why S.E.L.L. I.T.?

Through each step in the process, your ideal outcome is addressed and checked in with. Often at the beginning of your journey you have an idea of what you expect from the future.

You have an idea of how much your business is worth. It may not have any basis in reality but it's the number you've got in your head. Perhaps you have been thinking about what's next in your life after work? I know many business-owners can't imagine what they'll do with themselves as their company has consumed their entire lives for so long. Others have hobbies, holidays and adventures planned with no specific date when they are going to do them.

Through the S.E.L.L.I.T. process you build up to achieving what you really want for yourself, your life and your business. There is enough flexibility built into the process for there to be changes to the road map at key points in time.

Transparency on what comes next and what is involved means you are in control of the process rather than feeling like you are on a roller-coaster. Most business-owners experience a lot of ups and downs when they go on the selling journey.

You'll notice that the first two elements are planning, which might seem like a lot of planning. Getting out of your business is a BIG goal, not a flippant decision you make today and complete by the end of the week, especially if you are involved in the day-to-day management. Prepare for significant disruption to the flow of activity.

You can't do it alone. You must involve others who may not currently be equipped to pick up the reins straight away. Planning saves you time and money. It could be worth millions to you by the end of the process. Not planning WILL cost you thousands (possibly millions) and change the outcome you achieve, not for the better.

Planning gives you transparency on your business road map. It gives you clarity on who is involved and their role in the process. You can spend time engaging with the right people, taking care to engage with advisors that understand you and your business.

Often the exit process is defined, for the business-owner, by the feeling of being out of control.

PART 2

Succession Planning

"Succession Planning often results in the selection of a weaker representation of yourself."
Peter Drucker

Why do you need a succession plan?

There is a 100% chance that you will leave your business one day, sometime in the future. When that will be is anyone's guess.

The one thing that business owners tend to forget is that they aren't immortal. Let's face it, not just business owners forget this. Over 50% of business owners leave their business because of unplanned circumstances – death, disease, disability and, sometimes, divorce. The first 3 are the big ones. How well equipped you leave your business has an enormous impact on the future value of it. It's worth asking "What would happen if I wasn't able to work?"

Effective succession planning makes sure a company always has the right team in place just in case there are any unexpected changes, especially to the leadership.

Failing to plan for succession leaves your business worth less and in some cases that can mean literally worthless. Succession planning builds in resilience and adaptability. A succession plan is good insurance against the unexpected and, while it is time-consuming there are significant benefits for your business:

Risk Management

Succession planning is the equivalent of an insurance policy for your business. You have no idea what might happen tomorrow – to you or your family – so having a backup plan is worthy of the effort. Equally you might have a great team right now but what happens if one of your key employees decides to go to Tibet to "find himself" or leave to set up their own business. You can't stop them leaving but you can be ready.

Think of succession planning as maintenance for your business, in the same way that an airline always maintains their aircraft even though they very rarely crash. With succession planning you are looking for the next leaders in your business and spending time getting them ready for when they need to step up.

Increases Employee Engagement

Engaging with employees and letting them know there is a plan for their progress encourages them to share their aspirations with you.

Employees can decide whether that is the route they wish to pursue and develop new skills in advance of the change in role. It's a great motivation and retention tool which cuts your recruitment costs if you get it right.

If your existing team has no wish to progress or they simply don't have the skills and attitude, you can make plans for external recruitment. With a succession plan you know what you are going to need in terms of people and how to invest in your existing team to develop them into the roles they aspire to.

Succession planning goes hand in hand with in-house mentoring and development of employees. As junior members of the team are developed into senior roles, they can ask questions about how things work – and why. This means that there is a review of processes and procedures through challenge and questioning and junior members of staff bring new insight into the organisation's established practices.

Reinforces Company Culture

When you recruit from within you are reinforcing the company culture, behaviours, and legends. The caution here is to reinforce positive cultures. Whilst there are benefits to bringing in "new blood", maintaining values and being dialled into the purpose or mission of the business is often easier from within.

Strategic Planning

If you build a succession plan, the chances are you are looking at all the strategic aspects of your business. You'll also engage with your employees at a level that is not normal in most small and medium size businesses (or many large ones for that matter). Communication with your employees on all matters is one of the keys to success.

With a strategic plan which sets out goals and targets that are communicated to your team, you are already in the top 20% of all businesses. With a team who understand what they need to do to have a positive financial impact on the business and how achieving it affects them, you'll have a business that is worth more and give you and them a richer, happier future.

Creating a career development path for employees to take over from their senior colleagues means years of hard-earned knowledge about the business won't walk out of the door if there are retirements, leavers or, at worst, unexpected events of a more tragic nature.

A succession plan helps your company grow while you reduce vulnerabilities in the business, improve process, encourage innovation, develop team potential, and reduce employee turnover.

Who is the next leader?

One of the most important aspects of choosing the next leader in your organization is understanding what you are looking for. If you are honest with yourself, you were probably not the best leader for your business once you got it past the initial startup phase.

As businesses go through the various stages of growth, they need different skills and knowledge to allow them to grow and thrive. Many businesses are kept at a ceiling because of their structure and the capacity and capability of the people leading them.

"True leaders practice the 3 Rs – respect for self; respect for others and responsibility for their actions."

A classic example of this is the 30-year-old business that has been unable to exceed £2m turnover because of the stranglehold on leadership by the shareholders. Every time the business expanded to exceed the effective span of control of the owners, things would start to fall apart. The business would shrink back for a few years then grow again. Rinse and repeat over the decades.

During all the expansion and contractions, the business was not building on sustainable, solid foundations and remained reliant on the business owners. Many CEOs have been and gone over the years, most lasting no more than 2 years before being worn out from the battle of trying to establish processes and make the business owners redundant.

It was only the impact of aging that made the owners realise that they could not go on forever and they were relying on the business for their retirement funding. Now in their 70s they are taking the active steps towards removing themselves from the day to day and letting their team take the reins.

It's not without the odd hiccup as old, established behaviours rear their ugly heads and the business takes a step backwards. Now they are measuring not just profitability but capital value, their bad behaviour can be measured in value damage which is a very effective way to manage it.

They also know what it takes to run a bigger company and they are making the choice to not be part of the leadership team so the structures can be put in place.

A £1m turnover business with 10 employees needs a very different set of skills to a £100m turnover multi-national organization with 10,000 employees. In an ideal world the people you started out with would all stay for the growth journey and be able to step up into the senior management roles as they developed with the business. But that's not what happens.

The people who are great at start-ups, do everything because there is no one else to do it and stay to get that customer order out no matter what are very rarely the same people who can handle a business with external investors and multiple layers of management.

In family businesses especially it can be a default that the eldest child takes over the company. This might explain why there are only 1 in 25 family businesses that last 4 generations. Age and position in the family hierarchy is not the best indicator of leadership success.

So how do you find the next leaders?

There are entire libraries written on leadership that can cover this far better and, in more depth, than I can. See references and reading lists for more.

To get started in thinking about this meaty subject, here's a few ideas on how to find the leaders in your business:

Look for potential in passion

Anyone in your team who is driven by passion might be exhibiting all the characteristics of the next leader, though they may be a bit rough around the edges. With potential and passion there are training and development opportunities.

Get a coach or mentor into the business

If you have several people who have great future potential, then getting a coach or mentor to guide them into their full capabilities is a worthwhile investment of time, money and energy. The most unlikely potentials are unlocked in a mentoring or coaching program.

Offer job rotation

Job rotation is where employees from different areas of the business spend time doing each other's jobs. It can be a day, week or months and has a positive impact on team building or breaking down silos in a business.

When I joined the Wrens in the 1980s, a junior WRNS officer did a 6-month rotation as a junior Wren before starting officer training. It was a great way of gaining insight into what a rating faced in daily life. It was literally walking in the shoes of the people you would eventually command.

Baroness Karen Brady uses job exchange and rotation as part of her business practice to make sure that all employees do at least 2 days job rotation every year. She's got this working at West Ham Football Club to great effect. Not for players on match days I must emphasise, though sometimes with the results you might wonder.

In other organizations I have implemented multi-week job rotations to great effect not just from identifying leadership potential but also for building better performing teams and improved business processes.

"Train people well enough so they can leave, treat
them well enough, so they don't want to."
Richard Branson

Ask your team "who" they would want as a future leader. This might seem obvious but asking other people in your organization who they like working with and why can bring up some interesting observations. In a positive and encouraging culture it's a great method of gaining insight. In a poor culture it's an offer to bitch and moan about other employees.

Building a team

"I don't have a leadership or management team!" I hear some of you cry. Or you don't have the right team, which is more common.

No successful entrepreneur has ever built something bigger than themselves without the aid of a supportive and talented team. That doesn't stop it being lonely at the top – being an entrepreneur can be just as lonely whether you have 1 or 100 staff.

Successful entrepreneurs weave together a collection of the right skills and attitudes to enable their businesses to become greater than the sum of their parts. Whilst founders may be the ones who take the first brave steps, it is their ability to recruit followers, supporters and challengers that keeps their businesses in the top %.

Ideas are cheap, action is the critical factor in getting those ideas into reality and delivered, repeatedly and consistently. All the biggest and most successful companies have a mix of different characters, inspiring an army of talented people who help turn an idea into reality.

Building a Team to Scale

Despite all the evidence that a team is essential to business growth and success, many business owners simply do not "staff up" effectively or quickly enough to grow their businesses. It is important to find the skills and talent for each activity in the business – from administration, finance, sales, and marketing to customer service.

Doing it all yourself means you are going to get tied up in what I call £10 per hour work instead of £10,000 per hour work. It makes no sense to spend hours doing your own bookkeeping if you can get it done quicker and more effectively by someone you pay £15 per hour to – thus releasing you to spend those hours getting sales, negotiating contracts, or building a strategy that grows your business.

Yes, some jobs won't be done exactly how you do them – but they might be done better or differently OR both!

But what about the cost?

One of the barriers to recruiting staff is the way business owners perceive the cost of employing expensive team members. Once you have considered what additional staff do in your business and you are clear what value they add, then it's a matter of viewing it as an investment.

Is it different with a permanent fulltime employee? - NO!

Regardless of how you employ additional members of your team, they all need to be paid whether that's by invoice or through payroll. If you are earning more than it is costing you in the hours you now have free, you are investing in the growth of your business.

And what if it doesn't work out?

Even if you are employing personnel directly, they are always on a trial period when they first start. Making your recruitment processes rigorous should avoid most problems but there is always the odd person who just doesn't fit no matter how well they interview or look good on paper.

That's why there are probation periods in your contracts of employment (if there aren't, get some added!).

Your investment is not the annual wage, it's only the amount of money you need to pay until the new employee becomes effective or you find out they don't fit. Be slow to hire and quick to fire to make sure you get and keep the right people. It's more important to get rid of anyone who isn't right. Don't be afraid to make decisions. I've seen too many business owners make themselves AND THEIR STAFF miserable by not firing someone that isn't right for the business.

Building a team and delegating to them allows your business to THRIVE.

There are 4 key steps for getting started:

- Get the right essential talent in your in-house team.

- Use freelancers and contractors for specialist activities that are not part of your core offer.

- Collaborate with partners, affiliates, and joint ventures to extend your reach.

- COMMUNICATE.

If you are serious about having a business that's worth more, then there is more on this subject in the reading list.

Exit Ready

"Failure is the road you will travel to success; just be sure you take the correct exit."

Tim Fargo

What is exit readiness?

You might not be thinking of selling your business right now but there is a 100% guarantee that you will leave your business at some point in the future. The only debate is whether you'll be in control of the process – or not.

From personal experience, I know that most business owners have not considered their exit timeline and have an unrealistic view of how much time they need. It's estimated that nearly 90% of baby boomer business owners do not have a written exit plan.

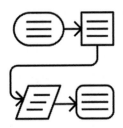

Business owners are simply too busy or are unaware of how vital exit planning is to sell a company. Every business owner eventually faces the decision of what to do with his or her company. When they decide the time is right, they need to be fully informed about the M&A process.

If you are like most entrepreneurs your biggest assets are two items:

1. Your home
2. Your business

Chances are good that your entire retirement depends upon what you do with these two items.

Being as exit ready as possible adds value to your business as well as de-risking the investment you've made into what is probably your biggest financial asset. The more your business relies on you being there, the less it is worth to a potential buyer or investor, including if you are considering a management buy-out or employee ownership.

Exit planning is an on-going process not a single event.

Exit planning is one of the most neglected areas of business risk management, which is surprising given the number of business owners who are reliant on the value they can release from their business to fund their retirement.

Lack of knowledge about the sale or ownership transfer process means that most businesses are poorly prepared for the exit of their owners. The owner is usually equally unprepared and avoids thinking about "what's next" and gets busy reacting to the day to day needs of the business.

Being ready for the unexpected is as important as being prepared for planned activity. The value of a business is based on more than the numbers (I know I keep saying this but it's worth repeating because it is so easily forgotten). It's the non-financial aspects of a business that makes deals fall apart when the due diligence process gets started.

Exit readiness means preparing your business so that a buyer finds it an attractive investment in the future. The more attractive, the higher the value.

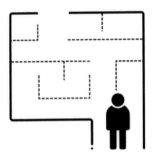

"Every exit is an entry somewhere else."
Tom Stoppard

Understanding the Essentials

Most business owners only sell one business in their lifetime, and few have a clear understanding of the process before embarking on the journey.

One of the most important factors to remember is that being exit ready does not mean you have to be thinking about selling or transferring ownership right now. Being exit ready protects the value in your business AND shows that you are considering the impact of an unplanned event. It's something your family, employees and customers will thank you for if something unexpected happens to you that affects your capacity to run the business.

Having an effective shareholder agreement, a buy / sell agreement and the appropriate insurance in place are some of the essentials to arrange immediately if you don't have them already in place.

When a business owner starts to think about selling, it's often while they start looking for someone to help them with the transaction. They'll take recommendations from friends or peers, but they rarely address the issues that may reduce the value of their business before getting M&A advisors to help with selling.

This frequently leads to finding a broker who takes fees regardless of success. Beware of those brokers in the market who

66

declare how many businesses they have sold – a better question is what percentage of the clients that come to you, have you actually achieved a sale for?

But before we get ahead of ourselves, let's look at what the essential requirements a buyer looks for in a business that makes the sale get across the line. Remember nearly 80% of all businesses that 'go to market' never get sold. There are 4 parts to getting exit ready:

1. Explore the options

2. Understand the journey

3. Get your business valued

4. Take the actions to move the current value to your expectations

Knowing Your Weaknesses

If you know what a buyer is going to find when they undertake due diligence, you're prepared for it – or better still you can take the actions that add the most value.

There is no point in thinking that you can hide the weaknesses in your business because the due diligence (DD) process picks everything apart to find them. If not found in the DD, they are covered in the Sale and Purchase Agreement (SPA) with the warranties and indemnities.

By knowing what's good and what's not the best in your business, you're able to focus your time, energy, and money on improving the things that make the most difference and add the most value. Or you're fully aware of what value you are leaving on the table when you sell.

I always think of business performance as a graphic equaliser. Some of the buttons are up at 8, 9 or 10 whilst others are down at 2, 3 or 4. Making sure the highs stay high is good but raising the lows up a point or two makes a big impact. Going from 2 to 4 is doubling performance and probably taking a lot less effort than moving 8 to 9.

Being P.E.R.F.E.C.T.

Getting ready for exit is a big job and covers every aspect of the business. Some of the elements we've covered in the Succession Planning chapter.

To keep focused on exit planning specifically, there are 7 key essential elements to being prepared.

- Profitability

- Employees

- Reliance on owner

- Financial forecasting and reporting

- Efficiency

- Corporate Governance

- Timing

Profitability

When a potential buyer looks to acquire another company, their view of profitability may be from a different perspective to the seller. All profits are not equal.

Buyers are generally looking for one or more of 3 things from an acquisition:

- Capacity - adding the ability to scale, grow and serve more customers
- Capability - adding new or more advanced skills to the overall business
- Access to customers - adding customers so you can sell a wider range of products or access a new market more easily than starting from scratch

Whichever is their priority changes their view of the business and its risks. If they are looking for capacity and scalability then they need to see that the infrastructure of the business is in place to do that OR be prepared to invest more funds in creating it. The amount of investment required for the future changes their view on the value of the business now.

Evidence of planning for the future always plays well with investors and buyers (and lenders for that matter). It shows awareness within the business of what's possible and what the business owner has been thinking about. If this adds to evidence of sustainable growth and taking advantage of new opportunities, then value is added to the business. Execution of plans is even better. Plans mean nothing without actions.

Buyers take a look at all aspects of the various relationships your business has with customers, suppliers, competitors etc. Each rank in a different order of importance depending on the lens with which the buyer is viewing the investment they are about to make.

All buyers look at the risks involved. It's worth using the Porters' 5 Forces model to look at your business risks, strengths, and weaknesses:

Figure 1. Porters 5 Forces

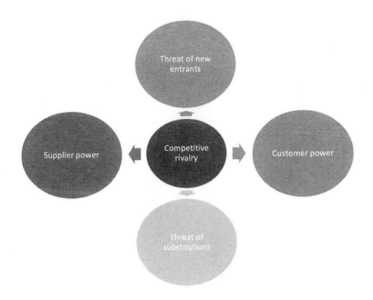

Your ability to address these risks appropriately keeps the deal on track through the due diligence process. They are all factors that should be part of your regular strategic review and board meetings. If they aren't now, then it's a good time to get them on to the agenda so that future buyers can see you really paid attention to them.

Employees

Within an autonomous business, the executive team has the responsibility and authority to make decisions. The best performing teams have the same mindset as an owner, and this is usually supported by appropriate incentives and engagement. The business directors and managers who operate a business as if it were their own make decisions for the long-term value of the business as well as the immediate profitability.

Your succession plan is key to getting the right senior management team in place. See chapter 6 for more insight. Mitigating the reliance on a single or few individuals is a significant component of your succession plan.

Reliance on Owner

One big truth in business, the more the owner works IN the business, the less the business is worth. A business that relies on the owner brings with it inherent risks for the next owner.

A business that is autonomous is a more attractive investment because the next owner won't need to worry about what happens if the owner disappears on a world cruise or worse (death, disability, disease etc).

Financials

Chaotic businesses do not forecast their performance and rarely have a working strategic plan in place. High performing businesses have both and actively set strategic plans which are communicated to their employees and allow their senior management team to make effective decisions.

Efficiency

Business efficiency is all about processes. A process is simply any input that is changed into an output. A system is a set of processes that work together to complete a complex whole.

Systems are not just IT! Information technologies are the tools that can be used to effectively operate and automate routine and repetitive processes. Advances in Artificial Intelligence and Machine Learning are allowing businesses to reduce the impact of the Human Factor (errors or inconsistency caused by varying levels of competence or boredom).

Systems in the context of efficiency refer to processes, procedures, and methods of working that allow a consistent high quality of delivery for repetitive or repeatable tasks or decision-making. Some are automated and once set up can be set in motion following certain triggers. Some are tasks and guidelines for human operation, making sure that each task is designed to give the same outcome regardless of who delivers it.

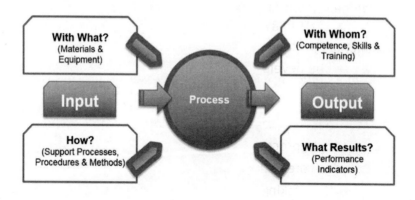

The benefit of "systems" is that you as the business owner can extend your influence and reach by showing others how to do increasingly complex tasks so that you can get on with more complex or higher-level tasks. Building a set of processes and written procedures allows you to scale your business more effectively without reducing quality.

Processes allow teams of specialists to work more effectively together and improve efficiency.

There are three types of process:

- Management processes

- Operational processes

- Support Processes

Each has a different function, and they all work in a hierarchy. Management processes focus on planning and are strategic. For example, if a strategy is agreed to develop a new product, the management process would be the planning to organise how the product will be developed and then the routes and timescale to market.

Operational processes are the tasks and steps required to delivery your core product / service delivery. This will include everything from taking the order, manufacture, or preparation of services though to final delivery and after care.

Support processes are all the activities required to make the other processes as friction free as possible. For example, taking on new staff, making payments to suppliers, making sure IT works etc.

How your business has behaved has an impact on your business value. A past littered with late payments, errors in statutory returns and fines for non-compliance is a sign of a disorganised business. It's a visible clue as to what is hiding behind the closed doors of the business. Buyers see this as a risk and reduce the price they are willing to pay as a result.

During a sale process you are required to make declarations about the levels of compliance on all aspects of the company from taxes to health and safety. Any potential future liability arising because of past activity is usually covered in the Sale and Purchase Agreement in the form of warranties and indemnities. This can often result in funds being held in escrow or being held back for a period IN ADDITION to a price reduction.

Well run businesses have a board of directors who understand directors' duties, obligations, and liabilities. As a business grows, it is advisable to have independent director level input either as a non-executive director or independent business advisor who isn't line managed by the owner (for example) and therefore isn't afraid to ask difficult questions.

Timing

One of the major factors in business success is TIMING! Changes in the economy, in technology, in social attitudes all influence the outcomes for your business.

Bill Gross gave a TEDx talk on business success factors in 2015. He wanted to find out why so many failed! He wanted to know what influenced success. He did an analysis of 100s of Start-Ups and was surprised by the outcomes.

He used to think that the IDEA was the key, though he also looked at the TEAM, the BUSINESS MODEL, levels of FUNDING and TIMING. Having looked at 200 companies, he judged that for 42% of all the companies, TIMING was the biggest factor in their success. This was followed by TEAM at 32%. Surprisingly FUNDING was the last factor in the list.

No one can ever be completely certain about timing for the market BUT you can be certain what's good timing for you, your life, and your family. Getting exit ready means you can leave when you want to without leaving money on the table and your business is easier to sell on better terms. It is never going to be wasted time, effort, or money.

"Ask any comedian, chef or tennis player,
timing is everything."
Meg Rosoff

It's a good time to ask questions that an investor asks and be prepared for it. That process alone might uncover hidden value in your business that you are blind to for being too close to it.

Now is the best time to address how you value your intellectual property, for example. What's your "secret sauce"? Is it the patentable product, licensable service, or your unique processes? Recognising these early and capitalising on them by documenting them adds value to your business. Many businesses simply do not pay enough attention to their intellectual property to document it because they think it's "normal".

One way to reduce the risks perceived in your business is operating from multiple locations or showing expansion opportunity including unexplored export potential. Having these growth possibilities makes your business attractive to buyers who can exploit them either with more investment or by utilising their existing position.

Explore the Options

An exit journey is not a single path. It's more like the choices your satnav gives you when you plan a trip where you'll be given the fastest route, the simplest route and the route that avoids motorways or toll roads.

Most business owners have a multitude of options available to them when it comes to transfer of ownership. This isn't clearly understood by most business owners, and it is not explored by some brokers who are not motivated to educate their clients.

A good broker or M&A advisor makes sure you understand your choices and what alternatives are available to you.

As the combination of options is so varied, I'm going to cover the general principals here but there are resources and further reading later in this book and you can always just give me a call! A 30-minute conversation illuminates what's possible and gives you more insight than you have now.

What are the options? Here's a few ideas – it's not an exhaustive list and I have left out 'closing the doors' which is also an exit option:

- Transfer within the family

- Buy-out from other shareholders

- Become employee owned

- Management Buy Out

- Sell to a third party (this has multiple options within it)

- Merge with a competitor or adjacent industry

- Buy another company (which sounds counter intuitive)

- Get a public listing (IPO)

- Sell only part of your ownership

- Get investment from Private Equity or Venture Capital

Each of these options does not exclude any of the others, in fact you may choose a combination of them to get to your final destination.

As a business owner the best time to look at your options is as early as possible. You can explore on paper, the potential outcomes and prepare for the one that best suits you and your business. It may change over time. You may start out thinking you will sell to the highest bidder and then decide that you are going to become an employee-owned company. If you are a family business, the intention may be to pass it on to the next generation. If the next generation are not interested, then you must look at other options and prepare accordingly.

One thing is certain:

100% of business owners leave their business, one way or another.

The only thing up for debate is how ready you are when it happens and how much control you have.

Understand the journey

With so little understanding of the exit process, it is no wonder that business owners get frustrated with the elements of the journey they are about to undertake.

Selling your business is a hard journey, both mentally, emotionally, and physically. If you aren't prepared it is going to take its toll on you and may end up without a transaction to show for all the effort and anxiety.

You're going to end up with fees to pay even if the transaction fails. But this is not the only price to pay. The disruption to your business has future impacts too, often in lost revenue, lost staff, and reduced efficiency for a period of time.

In more than one case I have joined a business where the broker is already involved, and the sale process has become stuck. In almost all cases the issue could have been addressed if the business owner had been given a clear idea of the steps in the process and what was needed in terms of preparation. It's the equivalent of making sure your car is full of petrol for a long trip.

I'm going to summarise the journey here and go into more detail on the individual steps in later chapters. It's worth knowing the general direction of your journey before delving into the actions you need to take. The headlines of an exit journey are:

- Preparing your business for the exit option you have chosen

- Finding the right advisors

- Writing a brochure explaining your business to a buyer

- Finding a buyer

- Undertaking buyer due diligence (there is also seller due diligence)

- Preparing the transaction documentation

- Negotiating the final details

- The transfer of ownership

- Post transaction requirements and commitments

To get into the right frame of mind you need to start looking at your business through a buyer's lens. Attracting a buyer is very much like finding customers, you must give them what they are looking for, which means understanding what they are seeking from the acquisition of your business. The first issue is getting your business professionally valued.

"Before everything else, getting ready is the secret to success."
Henry Ford

Letting Go

"Don't cry because it's over, smile because it happened."
Dr Seuss

Why is Letting Go a Challenge?

You built your business from scratch or at least you were there in the early days of its birth. And that brings a bond that many employees just don't understand.

Starting a business is hard, selling it is harder

The hardest part of setting up your own business is actually "starting". You had the original idea, that morphed into something else and finally took shape as a "possibility"! Then you did what so many fail to do, you took the first tentative step towards just doing it.

You overcame the FEAR. You overcame perceived barriers to success, and you were willing to take the risks required to get the life you want. But anyone who is going into business for themselves heeds the wise words of those who have boldly gone before them – and I'm not talking about "Beam me up, Scottie!"

Business ownership is hard work, requiring commitment and resilience. It's not for the faint hearted – but you don't need to be superman or wonder woman. You need to define your own idea of success and make your own goals, not someone else's. You make mistakes along the way and learn from them rather than be afraid of making them.

Most of all you need to take control of the biggest barrier - the 7 inches between your ears.

Success is largely about mind-set. So is letting go!

Starting the business is the first commitment and it sets in motion a bond between you and your business that over time generally becomes stronger and stronger. The longer you are in your business the harder it becomes to see your business with the detachment required to sell it. In fact, the very characteristics that got you started in business are the characteristics that hold you back at the other end of your business journey.

"Time is one of my most valuable assets."
Bill Anderson

Getting mentally detached from the day to day of your business is the first step to letting go, and it's the hardest part but well worth it because the more you work IN your business the less it's worth.

Just to illustrate how difficult letting go is, I want to share a conversation I had just this morning with a client. The 2 business owners had built the business from scratch and over 10 years had been on the roller coaster of entrepreneurship. Both worked in and on the business, more in than on.

Over a couple of years, we'd had several conversations about recruiting staff and how to make sure they got the right people. Yet every time they would recruit as cheaply as possible and then complain about the quality of the person they hired until that person left. In their mind it justified their thinking. One year they hired a digital marketing specialist at, to their mind, a very high daily rate. The daily rate was significantly lower than his normal corporate rate, so he negotiated a bonus on any upside he generated for them. Performance related pay at its most basic.

At first their reaction was "OMG we'll be paying him thousands" without considering that the benefit to them would be significant increases in their dividends. Eventually they figured out a deal that worked for both. He effected incoming marketing that doubled their turnover in one year. They considered ending the contract because he was too expensive when they looked at how much he ended up earning. They didn't consider the fact that their personal income had more than doubled, they focused on how much he earned compared to them as business owners.

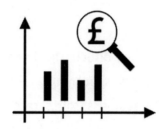

When discussing preparation for sale and reducing owner reliance, it was a well-worn conversation that the business couldn't operate without them and everyone they got in was rubbish and let them down.

In the same conversation they also said, "We're hiring an apprentice, I'm sure that an apprentice can do most of what we do". It was such a contradiction in one conversation. It illustrates the Jekyll and Hyde aspects of being a business owner who has a "job" in the business.

The idea of letting go of the control completely scared them yet they didn't see how investing in hiring the right skills would add value. Whilst at the same time seeing that part of what they did as a day job was skilled and needed someone with experience to take over. The more they worked in their business the more they thought it was worth. The exact opposite is true. Their challenge is separating the 3 roles they have in their business.

If you make most of the decisions in the business, then the buyer doesn't see you as ready for sale. To mitigate the risks a new buyer often wants some contingencies covered in the deal. This may involve an earn out. Having a management team that is empowered to make decisions reduces the perception of risk. It may remove the requirement for you to remain with the business after the sale.

When you produce detailed forecasts for future growth that buyers rely on in their price calculations these form the basis for earn-out clauses in the sale contract. If the forecasts become reality earn-outs reward buyers and sellers.

The 3 roles of a business owner

An owner commonly has 3 roles in the business. They own it, they direct or control it and they work in it.

The 3 roles are bundled together both in activities and mentally. They are so welded together they become one identity for the business owner. The longer the identities are bundled together, the harder it is to create any form of separation. As you build your team, they see the behaviour of the business owner acting in all 3 roles without being able to see any separation.

The team behaviour then reinforces the 3 merged roles with their tolerance of the business owner's behaviour. This appears in the everyday acceptance that, while the working day is 9-5.30, if you are the boss, you can roll in at 10am. Even if the owner is acting in a job role.

With no transparency in the roles, the team see it as one rule for us and another rule for "them".

A company joins the actions of 3 groups of people – shareholders, directors, and employees. The first step to understanding what impact the roles have on the value of the business is being clear on what is the purpose of each role.

Ownership / Shareholder

As a shareholder, your role in the organization is to invest money in the share capital and receive a return from the trading profits. A shareholder's financial responsibility is restricted to the value of their capital investment. In small and medium size businesses the relationship between the shareholder and the business is often more complicated. More than money, there is time, effort, sacrifice and emotional investment in a business.

There are a few rights that a shareholder has. They include having access to company records, regular statutory meetings, voting rights etc. Most of the details are written in the Articles of Association or a shareholder agreement, if there is one. More details on a shareholder agreement can be found in Chapter 7.

If you are working in the business, as the owner, you're likely to be setting the culture and acceptable behaviours (especially what happens when you aren't there). Leadership comes from you and everything you do, whether you are aware of it or not. Everything that happens is your fault.

Shareholders define strategic goals for the business by investing in the resources to achieve them. They set the return-on-investment expectations by the dividends they want to receive.

Director

The board of directors are responsible for the management of the business. Directors make strategic and operational decisions as well as being responsible for keeping the company legal. Directors participate in board meetings and facilitate decision making.

The directors are appointed by the shareholders to manage its business's day-to-day affairs. Directors act together as a board but typically there is some delegation of powers to individual directors or board appointed committees i.e., managing director, CFO, remuneration committee and audit committee.

There is a difference between shareholders responsibilities and duties and those of directors. If you are in both roles, it is crucial that you understand the difference and can separate roles. Understand which role you are in at any one time. Being both a director and a shareholder removes some of the protection you can enjoy as a shareholder. Being a director has legal implications, which are often overlooked when signing up to be a director. As your company grows so do the liabilities.

A director has 7 key duties:

1. Act within their powers under the company's constitution (usually the articles of association).

2. Act in a way that they consider, in good faith, would be most likely to promote the success of the company for the benefit of its members (shareholders) as a whole.

3. Exercise independent judgement. Directors are meant to develop their own informed view on the company's activities.

4. It's the duty for directors to exercise reasonable skill, care and diligence in their role

5. Avoid or manage conflicts of interest which may affect their objectivity.

6. A director of a company must not accept a benefit from a third party

7. If a director of a company is in any way, directly or indirectly, interested in a proposed transaction or arrangement with the company, he must declare the nature and extent of that interest to the other directors.

Directors must also keep minutes of board meetings to provide a record of the board's decision-making process.

Employee

Employees have a responsibility to give a fair day's work for a fair day's pay. The employees are one of a company's main assets and biggest costs. When they know their roles and responsibilities and what is expected they generate much greater value than the sum of their parts.

Some are specific technical experts. All are expected to work together as a team to contribute to the business success by acting in the business' best interests using problem-solving and taking the right decisions. The challenge is when the business owner is the only decision maker, they become a bottle neck in the business.

The work culture is also part of the employee's responsibility. They must comply with the policies and regulations and respect one another in the workplace. Employees play a big role in all business activities including profitability. Business owners often get in the way of this without intending to, such as when they expect one type of behaviour and act differently themselves i.e., timekeeping.

Employees are required to obey the employment contract, reasonable orders, cooperate with the employer and serve in a faithful manner. They are also responsible not to divulge and misuse the confidential data of the organization.

Employees have rights as a matter of law.

Employees have a right to work in a safe and healthy workplace and they have a duty to make use of safety work equipment for protection. Employees are entitled to appropriate rest periods during the working day if their hours exceed legal minimums for a break. They are also entitled to annual paid holiday including bank holiday allowances and they can refuse to work during holiday periods and at weekends if these are not part of their contracted hours. On most employee contracts the working hours are fixed, exceeding these hours results in additional payments and benefits.

Workers have protection from unfair dismissal and can file a complaint to an industrial tribunal if they feel that they have been unfairly treated.

It's one of the biggest fears of an employer that if you have effective processes and the support of a good HR advisor, you're rarely going to experience the challenge of an industrial tribunal. The secret is robust policies and procedures, consistently applied ON EVERY OCCASION.

Ask yourself, as the owner, are you acting as a good employer? Does the team know when you are in shareholder mode, or the director role or being an employee?

Ownership Mindset and Ownership Thinking

Business owners act and think very differently to employees. For a business owner, their company is usually more than just a job, it's part of their identity.

The key difference is having skin in the game, which business owners have in spades. They are all in. Working to align the interests of the owners and the employees is a great way to develop an ownership mindset in the employee team.

The challenge is that most business owners do not communicate with their employees in a way that fosters an ownership mindset. They keep details and information to themselves. This is "ownership thinking" – looking after what's theirs to the exclusion of everyone else. Yet by sharing part of the ownership, even if only through share options, means the employees are dialled into the value of the company.

Management consulting firm Oliver Wyman Delta, in a white paper on Building Ownership Culture stated: "A true 'ownership culture' is one where employees feel a substantial, personal stake in the company's performance. It creates a situation in which behaviour is guided more by values than by rules; even when 'nobody is watching,' people treat each spending decision as if they were, in fact, the owner."

96

Of course, to do this employees need to understand the business, its performance and how that performance is measured. This isn't something that is easy for business owners to implement without having a shift in their own mindset from ownership thinking. When employees are given the chance to understand the business, they get the opportunity to make a positive impact for the business, and for themselves.

When employees are empowered to ask the right questions and make decisions based on what is best for the business and everyone in it, they perform at a higher level. Your business spends less on recruitment because the team builds and supports itself, weeding out any poor attitudes along the way. The team polices itself and steps up to the highest level of performance rather than sinking to the lowest common denominator.

"Having a bad boss is not your fault, staying with one is."
Nora Denzel

Preparing for what's next

There are a multitude of websites and sources for preparing financially for retirement. And if you've just sold your business, you've hopefully got the funds you need. How did you know what you needed?

Did you sell with no onward commitments to the business? If you are tied into an earn-out as part of your company sale, then you'll have one of two situations.

1. You have control over the factors included in the earn-out and you are more likely to earn whatever rewards are associated.

2. You are not in the position to control results and you risk the earn-out value.

It is advisable to understand the full implication of any earn-out responsibilities, authority, and control. Earn-outs are a common feature of M&A deals because it allows buyers to reduce the risk to themselves of reliance on a seller's forecasts of future growth and results. It holds the seller to account.

As the seller, it's important to set the criteria for the earn-out in detail and in writing, including:

- What financial and non-financial goals are conditional for the final pay-out,

- How long the agreement lasts for

- How the final numbers and activities are verified.

Non-financial goals can be harder to quantify, and it is important to detail how they are measured and what control you have over them.

Earn-outs are more challenging where you have no influence over the outcomes. This happens when the seller is either completely outside the business for the earn-out period or in a role that doesn't have control or authority over the metrics. The main mistake sellers make is not having verifying criteria for whether goals are being achieved or not.

If you have not had experience in buying and selling businesses, you may not be aware of the intricacies of an earn-out, so getting expert advice well before the actual transaction is essential to protect any deferred payments.

Having the money solves one problem, but the other is "what are you going to do with your time?" Most people struggle with having lots of free time and no clear purpose. Doing something meaningful adds to life satisfaction significantly.

Many business owners have their identity tied to their business and that means the work they do has meaning. When you start thinking about selling your business, you also need to start planning what you are going to do with your time. When you've worked very hard, with long hours and laser focus on your responsibilities, you tend not to have had made time for hobbies or other interests. You might be considering dusting off the golf clubs or getting your motorbike out of the garage – but after a while this might not provide a replacement for purpose to your day.

When you become a retiree, regardless of your age, you can feel like you lose your identity. But you are not what you do and can still contribute to meaningful activity. Keeping physically and mentally active are essential parts of a long fulfilling life.

"Only stepping out of old ruts will bring new insights."
Andy Grove

Legals

"Incorrect documentation is often worse than no documentation."
Bertrand Meyer

Getting the right lawyer

Selling your business is one of the most stressful and complex legal issues you are likely to experience in your lifetime, so it pays to get the right partner on your side for you and your needs.

Pre-planning for a sale saves you time, money, and stress, especially the legal aspects. Selling is not just about getting the right price; it also means addressing and mitigating any risks of future liability. The day you handover the keys and get the cash is rarely the last day of your interest in the business.

The early stages of preparing your business for sale is the time to be proactive. The best time to prepare is at the beginning of your business journey but I know from personal experience that there's plenty of other things on your mind when starting out.

You wouldn't think to get eye surgery from a heart surgeon, and it's the same with legal advice. Getting advice from a niche law firm that understands the sale and purchase process means you have the confidence that you are getting the best possible advice. This isn't a job for your high street generalist solicitor.

A good M&A lawyer advises you well before the sale process is in progress so that you know and understand the journey you are embarking on and what is required in terms of documentation. Too many business owners go into the process completely blind.

When finding legal advice, you need to check out how many transactions they've been involved with and that they have current knowledge, know-how and experience. This helps you structure the best deal for you AND get it over the line. Many sale transactions start but never complete because of lack of preparation or understanding of the process.

A deal may involve anything from a complex share sale to a simple transfer of assets. Getting the right level of support is critical to manage every aspect of the transaction and avoid you getting distracted from the business quickly and efficiently.

The Legal Documents

There are a lot of legal documents involved in a business sale. It is important that the legal documents are well drafted when you sell your company. It is wise to familiarise yourself with the documents and the process involved before starting the process.

Before you even think about selling your business, having a shareholder's agreement in place is one of the essentials (in my opinion). A shareholder agreement regulates decision making for the shareholders including voting rights, lock-down provisions, restrictions on transferring shares, or granting security interests over shares as well as "tag-along" and "drag-along" rights. All these rules ensure that everyone who is a shareholder is clear on what happens to the shares of the company should anything happen to one or more of the shareholders.

A shareholder agreement stipulates how a business ownership gets transferred and how the process is triggered. Setting this out in advance means all shareholders understand what's going to happen when the conditions are right for a sale process.

Before you disclose any information, you engage with a third party on a confidential basis and the first document you share is a Non-Disclosure Agreement (NDA). This ensures that all information you provide to a potential buyer is kept confidential. When the potential buyer is a competitor extra care is required.

Sometimes this document is also called a confidentiality disclosure agreement or confidentiality agreement.

If you are using a broker or corporate finance advisors then you sign an engagement or mandate letter, which sets out the agreement between the selling parties and the advisor. This gives the details of expected fees for work done including any success fee, exclusivity arrangements and milestones for the sale project.

Before you get to the Sale and Purchase Agreement (SPA), the first "contract" step in the selling process is the offer from the potential buyer. It's often called Heads of Term (HoT), a Terms Sheet or a Letter of Intent (LOI). The document is typically not legally binding and provides clarity to both sides with what's been agreed in principle and the intentions of both parties. It can be partially or fully legally binding agreement and, when it is, it shows much more commitment from the buyer. Be clear if it's legally binding with explicit wording in the document.

"Common sense often makes good law."
William O. Douglas

The HoT or LOI is put in place before the due diligence phase has started. In essence it's the template for the detail of the deal that allows both sides to move forward into the next steps. A Heads of Terms often has several versions until both parties are agreed.

This is the time to ask lots of questions and not make any assumptions. If in doubt, ask because this is the stage at which misunderstandings can be cleared up rather than create expensive problems later in the process. Whilst it is the buyer who prepares the term sheet, the details need to be agreed by both parties. It's a two-way process to make sure the seller knows what the buyer is expecting to buy and vice versa.

The "sale" contract is called a Sale and Purchase Agreement (SPA) because it is a joint contract between the parties who are selling and buying. It's comprehensive and includes provisions for holding back funds or getting funds back if something goes wrong. It's the final step of selling a business and is undertaken by the buyer and their legal advisors.

The contract includes the sale of shares, the price, any withheld amount (including reasons and how the withholdings are released), taxes, warranties, limit of liabilities of the sellers and indemnities. Getting the right lawyer pays dividends at this point because they ensure that crucial items like any earn-out, non-compete or tie-in periods and the commitment to warranties or indemnities are structured to suit you. Sometimes it's years after the business sale that these legal items come back to haunt you if you are not properly protected.

An additional part of the sale documentation involves regulations such as employment protection i.e., TUPE (transfer of undertaking and protection on employment) and searches related to property. You may also be required to acquire contract assignments, transfers for leases and property through the Land Registry. Who is expected to pay the associated legal fees on this activity is included in the HoT.

Your employees are legally entitled to have their employment contracts transferred. You can't just make some of them redundant before a transaction to get the headcount down at the request of the buyer. Equally their terms and conditions cannot be materially adversely altered after the transaction either. If you have employees that shouldn't be working in your business, then act before the sale process or pay the price in reduced sale value.

And don't forget about restrictive covenants. These are the clauses that prevent you from taking certain actions after the sale such as setting up in competition for a period afterwards. Poaching staff often comes into play here too.

It might feel that you've got to the end of the paperwork mountain and then another piece of red tape is needed to be unlocked. Take heart that it does eventually come to an end.

What to prepare for

The sale process is poorly understood by most business owners before and often during the transaction. Here's the headlines and what you should know in advance.

Due Diligence

The due diligence stage is the most difficult and stressful part of the process. This is when the buyer and their team get to look under the bonnet of your business. They are going to ask questions about everything in your business to enable them to understand your company and its operations, it's strengths and weaknesses.

What they uncover exposes elements of risk that they may be unhappy with, and which can be used as an opportunity to reduce the offer price, request withholding amounts, or even withdraw their offer.

Your preparation and understanding of your business gives you a return on the investment of time and effort.

How long does it take?

Ask any business broker how long it's going to take, and they invariably answer, "it depends." Critical factors include your exit readiness, market conditions, industry sector, seller expectations and timing. The most common delays are caused by the sellers' lack of preparation. This includes not having the right team in support and trying to do it all yourself.

No business owner has ever regretted starting the preparation early.

Typically, most advisors in the M&A field say 9 – 12 months between signing a broker and handing over the business. And that's if the business is already prepared for going to market, which can take anything from 12 to 36 months depending on the state of the business.

The larger and more complex the business being sold, expect it to take longer than 12 months. It's important to remember that getting an offer does not guarantee completion for the deal.

It's a lot like buying a house – there are a lot of moving parts and multiple reasons for the deal to stall.

Doing a pre-sale due diligence process on your business, especially from an independent third party, allows you to see your business from the buyer's perspective and make adjustments that retain and increase the value of your business. Making it more likely you can complete the process.

Buyers often pay for the business using external finance, which takes time to put together. It's important to check out how the buyer is funding the purchase as early as possible and see some evidence of their ability to complete the purchase before wasting your time and effort on DD. There is no point negotiating with someone who can't pay!

Take your time when agreeing terms. Taking it slow at the beginning allows you to go faster at the end.

Understand that selling a business is difficult

Never underestimate how much energy and effort it takes to sell a business. It consumes you emotionally too. It is a test of patience and endurance.

Common Mistakes

There are some common mistakes people make in DD, even seasoned professionals. It's such a detailed look at your business that sometimes it's easy to lose sight of the big picture and get

109

engrossed in the weeds. Magnifying risks is one of the outcomes of this kind of behaviour.

Assessing the culture and environment of the business often gets lost yet has significant financial impact when it comes to post-acquisition integration. Being aware of the internal dynamics and behaviours within a business can be as important as the numbers.

On-site experience of the business in action is a great way to see how it works in real life as opposed to how it presents on paper. Buyers want to see the business in motion. This poses a challenge if your team do not know what's going on. In the absence of you telling them, they come to their own conclusions and make it up.

By focusing on risk mitigation, it can be easy to overlook potential and opportunities available. As a seller they may seem obvious to you but won't necessarily be obvious to the buyer unless you point them out. If you've got opportunities, then sign post them – they add value!

Equally if the DD team focus on opportunities, they can lose sight of some of the risks. DD is a balancing act for both buyers and sellers.

Intellectual property (IP) is covered in other chapters. Paperwork for this is not a 5-minute job. Preparation means taking action which leads to value and more cash in your pocket. Be especially careful if your business has licences for other peoples' IP that needs to be assigned or even renegotiated. Doing it in the DD phase is going to leave you on the back foot and possibly out of pocket. Get your trademark protection in place if applicable and make sure you own your website domain. Too many business owners find their domain is actually owned by their IT provider or web developer.

Getting contracts with suppliers and customers assigned generally only happens when the sale process is fairly well progressed. The first thing is identifying ALL the contractual relationships that need assigning. A good pre-due diligence process sweeps all this up, so you know what efforts are required to get the deal across the line and what legal fees are involved (and who is going to pay them). Assignments are also captured in the indemnity clauses of the SPA.

Taxes cannot be escaped. VAT, if you are VAT registered, particularly comes into play if you are selling assets as opposed to the entire business, which must remain a going concern. If in doubt, get tax advice and include VAT.

What does it cost?

Lawyers are one of your biggest bills. There is no legal requirement to have a lawyer act for you. You can do the whole thing without a lawyer, but it is not a route I would advise. Lawyers protect your interests now and in the future.

Costs vary enormously from £1000 per hour for big city firms to smaller boutique practices charging a lot less. Some solicitors work on a 1% of the transaction value as well as some fees, which can be negotiated on a fixed basis. The more prepared you are, the less your legal fees will be.

Of course, if DD shows some missing pieces there'll be the fees associated with putting them in place. Doing this last minute always costs more money. Don't forget you have to pay tax liabilities. And for tax advice. If money is held back in an escrow account, you'll need to think about the escrow costs too.

Preparation is key and it's never too early to start planning all aspects of this transaction.

Negotiating factors

The SPA has elements that confuse sellers as much as buyers. Here are some of the key parts of an SPA that may be new to you.

It's often when the first draft of the SPA is drawn up that a business owner comes across terms such as warranties, indemnities, conditions and escrow. Whilst this isn't an exhaustive list, here's some brief insights into these terms. As always if you are going through the sale process you are advised to get a good lawyer with M&A experience on board. This book is not a replacement for legal advice.

Warranties

Warranties provide protection to the buyer by a seller. Despite any amount of due diligence that the buyer does, they have ultimately relied upon information provided by or on behalf of the seller. Assumptions are made as a result.

Warranties provide one of a number of mechanisms to compensate the buyer if any information or assumptions is proven to be incorrect.

A warranty is an assurance of the condition of the business and can be either specific or implied (by law, for example). Warranties protect a buyer by providing a mechanism for adjusting the price or reclaiming funds from the final price paid. The seller becomes liable to pay compensation where a warranty is proven to be false and results in the buyer experiencing a loss. The onus is on the buyer to show evidence of such loss. The buyer also has the responsibility to mitigate losses incurred due to breach of warranty. The clear purpose of warranties is to ensure full and honest disclosure.

Indemnities

A subtle difference from a warranty, an indemnity is a promise to the buyer to reimburse any loss which they suffer because of a particular event or set of circumstances. The seller undertakes to indemnify (make good) a loss. The liability of the seller is dictated by how widely the parameters of the indemnities are drawn.

An indemnity provides guaranteed compensation to a buyer in circumstances in which a breach of warranty would not necessarily result in a claim for damages.

A claim under an indemnity is likely to be easier to establish than a claim for breach of warranty and there is no obligation for a buyer to mitigate its loss under an indemnity unless the contract expressly applies or excludes the rules on mitigation, remoteness, and causation.

Conditions

Conditions are the terms of a contract that are significant and if not performed or if breached mean the contract can be terminated. They are most used when regulatory approval is required. It should be noted that much like warranties, conditions can be implied by the law. A condition can protect both a buyer and a seller by ensuring that the parties are not obligated nor liable until the conditions have been fulfilled. Equally an innocent party can justifiably waive their right to treat the contract as terminated. This is likely to affect any claim for damages in the future.

A warning about delays

Warranties are statements of disclosure that are only true at the moment they are given. Understanding this is important if there is any delay between when the warranties are given and the completion of the contract. This is of special interest to the buyer, who may get last-minute disclosures if there are any changes in circumstances. As the seller you are advised to make complete, even last-minute disclosure of all relevant matters. Some sellers make late disclosures of material issues which, if on a tight completion timetable, a buyer is unable to properly consider. If you are tempted to do this (as a seller) don't be surprised if this results in further delays in the process by the buyer.

To ensure the seller is able to pay out indemnities or for breach of warranty, the buyer may require funds to be held in escrow for a period of time or for guarantees to be provided. Retention of part of the purchase price for a fixed period or a deferred payment of the sale price are also common.

The purpose of withholding or escrow funds is to make it easier for the buyer to receive claims that are successfully bought against a seller. Having a mechanism to claim is only worthwhile if the funds are available. Otherwise, a buyer may end up in protracted and potentially fruitless recovery processes and incurring more legal fees.

My experience of one exit was a sizable withholding fund resulting from the possibilities of pension liabilities AND the seller being an offshore resident. Two risks that meant that £6m was held in escrow for 6 years. No claim was made, and the funds were released to the shareholders in the appropriate time frame.

"Risk comes from not knowing what you are doing."
Warren Buffet

116

Information Memorandum

"Life is never quite like the brochure."
Chuck Lorre

What is it?

An information memorandum (IM) is your company's selling collateral, it's the headline factors that attract the perfect buyer for your business. Knowing who your potential buyer is means you can present the best IM to attract them.

The information memorandum (IM) is the first chance a buyer gets to see what your business is all about, especially if you aren't known to them through another relationship. You get this opportunity to present your business in the most positive light. Think of it as the application to a beauty parade where you'll be showing interested parties what an attractive investment prospect your business is. It's also the initial basis on which your eventual buyer considers putting in an offer so it's well worth spending some time and effort on getting the first impression pitched at the right level.

The message you send in your IM directs the type of buyer you attract. It is important to give an accurate and honest representation of all aspects of your business. Every IM is unique

117

and can vary widely from company to company, though there are always some common elements which buyers need to make informed offers. If these are absent, then no further expressions of interest follow:

- A description of the business and its history.

- The principal assets included in the sale.

- Summary current and historical financial information.

- Financial forecasts for the future (and their basis).

- Information about employees and, where appropriate, major customers and contracts.

A buyer is interested in how your company operates, and how you generate revenue. A summary of your products and services and the industry sector you operate in gives them an idea of whether they are looking at something of interest to them other than pure profit motive. Showing them your market awareness and understanding of the competitive landscape shows buyers that you understand the place your business occupies including its risks and its strengths.

"Information is only useful if it can be understood."
Muriel Cooper

Be clear on how you differentiate yourself from others in your market or industry and on your reasons for selling. Make sure it's clear what's for sale and what isn't, especially if there is property involved. A summary of your key staff is usually included and any contractual terms, especially if they are out of the ordinary (share options, special bonus arrangements) – though most of this is covered in minute detail in the DD too. The IM is the headlines.

Details of your major customers might be a step too far in the IM, but you need to tease the buyer with outline details of your customer base, including your typical customer type and any customers who are particularly important to the business.

Summary financial reports to illustrate the general financial health of the business are enough for most IM's. You don't need detailed analysis in the document, but you do need it for the DD.

More focus is usually given to summary forecasts for the future of the business. Do not be tempted to drift off into a fantasy land of "hopes and prayers" on your projections.

These need to be justified in the DD process and you should expect a lot of analysis on any projections.

Be guided by your professional advisors, but most IM's give an indication of the expected terms of sale and desired time scales for completion. Don't be afraid to set out what you want (or need). Yes, that might scare off some buyers, but it engages the ones who are willing and able to satisfy your requirements.

From experience keeping your IM clear, concise, and simple but impeccably accurate serves you better than complicated and full of holes. If your business is larger or more complex, then it's going to be longer and more detailed. The purpose of the IM is to generate interest enough to take potential buyers to the next step.

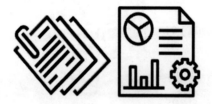

You need enough information to whet their appetite but not too much that could expose you to your competitors. IMs are usually very restricted in their distribution and only sent to interested parties after receiving a signed non-disclosure agreement (NDA). This gives you some legal protection against the information being disclosed without your express prior permission.

Do not be surprised by leaks. Sometimes they come about by accident especially if the process becomes protected. In one transaction a junior secretary on her first job for the M&A advisor had a single moment of indiscretion without realising she was in the presence of a financial journalist. The next day the deal was on page 6 of the Financial Times. In this case there was already a PR contingency plan in place. This was quickly enacted and the whole incident was managed positively to reduce the impact.

Having a PR plan in place and agreed with your team and advisors before anything happens is good preparation. It's always better to be on the front foot and lead in these situations.

Finding a buyer

No matter what your reasons for selling your business, finding a buyer requires a careful and strategic approach. Many sales processes never complete so choosing the right type of buyer is one of the critical steps.

There are so many more options available to business owners these days. With new financial instruments and lenders, more funding options, and an explosion of different private equity funds, it's just a matter of being fit to be acquired.

Buyers might be:

- Employees

- Competitors

- Suppliers

- Customers

- Employees of competitors

- Investor groups (private equity, venture capital, angel investment funds etc.)

- People looking to be an owner/operator

- Family or friends

In an earlier chapter we discussed a buyer acquiring for one of three reasons – capacity, capability, and access to customers. Potential business buyers also fall into three categories – strategic, financial and operators.

Strategic buyers are looking to join your business with an existing or curated portfolio of businesses that results in greater market share, synergies, or economies of scale, for example. It's all about building something that is greater than the sum of its parts and generates growth opportunities that can be leveraged. Strategic buyers are usually experienced and proficient at acquiring businesses.

Financial buyers are looking for investment gain usually through acquiring, improving and then selling businesses. This gives them a capital gain on the initial investment and the investment in improvements. Financial buyers such as private equity and venture capital are also proficient and savvy business acquirers.

Operator buyers acquire a business that they can operate and they usually own, direct, and work in the business they acquire. This includes employees looking to buy out through management buy-out or employee ownership vehicles such as Employee Ownership Trusts.

Finding the RIGHT buyer is very different from finding the buyers who pay the highest price. In the same way that not all potential house buyers are equal, not all business buyers are equal either. Qualifying a buyer before opening up your books to them is an important part of the journey.

Their offer is always going to be more than just the price.

Ask:

- What do I want out of the sale?
- How long will it take (i.e., what's the buyer timeline)?
- When will I get the money?
- Will I be tied in to an earn out?
- Can this buyer complete the deal (where's the evidence)?
- How serious is the buyer about completing the deal?

There are dozens of other questions you can ask depending on what you want out of it. Qualifying potential buyers in or out of the process early on is always worthwhile. Anyone really interested in buying filters you in or out of their process too.

Money is not the only thing you look for from the sale, you also want to consider other factors, such as:

- Your team – is the buyer providing opportunities for your company and your team to grow and improve?

- You – if you are on an earn-out and are staying in the company, do you like and trust the buyer. Do you see yourself working with them after the sale has completed?

- Your legacy – how would you feel if your buyer was going to break up your business and sell the assets?

- Employee ownership - Have you considered selling to your employees or having a management buyout?

Direct Approach

Occasionally a direct approach is made by a potential buyer that just fits everything you want from an acquirer, and you are a good a fit for them. This is a very rare occurrence and if it happens to you, then take the time to really celebrate.

There are also rare occasions where a buyer has been sitting in the background patiently waiting for you to make the decision to sell. They've made their intentions clear and just waited for the invitation to step forward and start the process. And along similar lines in family companies there is often a natural succession and transfer of ownership. Though from experience the transfer of ownership rather than management is often a contentious issue in family businesses. A subject for a completely different book, I think.

Finding a match

If none of these scenarios fit, then you need professional help finding a buyer. There are plenty of buyers out there but finding the one that's right for you is going to take research, time, knowledge, and energy. If you get it wrong, you end up with no buyer and your business reputation in tatters as your competitors get wind of the sale and start sowing seeds of doubt in the minds of your customers, suppliers, and staff.

Having successfully sold businesses by private invitation, through professional partners, I can recommend this route. You can use this method if you are doing it yourself. If you are industry aware then there are directories, trade press and information portals that allow you to research the market and reach out to prospective buyers to test their appetite. This is always best done through 3rd parties who find it infinitely easier to maintain your anonymity than if you are doing this on your own.

A good business broker or corporate finance advisor is worth every penny in fees. They handle every aspect of the sale for you including finding a buyer without you losing your anonymity until it's necessary. With professional support and advice, brokers act in your best interest and without emotional attachment. Most work on a fee plus commission basis, but it's worth every penny if they get your deal across the line with less pain, stress and usually for better terms than you would have negotiated for yourself.

Brokers find you a buyer through their own networks, research, and knowledge. They maintain confidentiality and manage the disclosure of your details when it's the appropriate time. They filter out the people who aren't committed buyers. Most of all a broker stops you becoming distracted from your business and avoids you getting embroiled in a potentially emotionally driven transaction.

Of course, you can find a buyer yourself. It's a lot like selling your own house. You think it will be easy, and you can save a lot of money. You get distracted from your business, you take a lot longer and you end up leaving more money on the table than you save. At a minimum, it's advisable to get your business valued so that you know how much to sell it for. If it's under-priced you lose thousands (if not millions), if it's overpriced you just won't sell.

Getting a third-party valuation gives you more confidence in your sale process by validating your offer to buyers. Sadly, most business owners have no idea how much their business is worth, and they never spend the time (or money) to find out.

98% of business owners have never had their business valued.

If you don't have an idea of your valuation, how do you know if a buyer is giving you the best value or not? A buyer is always going to undertake their own valuation before they part with their hard-earned cash.

If you have a lot of network connections, have been in your industry for a long time and have great insights or are well-known in your industry, you'll have a "black book" full of potential buyers.

Putting your head above the parapet and letting people know you are for sale is a challenge that is going to unsettle some people, including yourself. When your key stakeholders are nervous or uncertain this has a detrimental impact on the business. It's a tough dilemma.

You can't sell without letting people know you are available to buy. Equally keeping quiet guarantees no sale. With a third party marketing your business confidentially you maintain some distance from the process in the early stages.

If your staff hear rumours of a sale, they become unsettled. There are different thoughts on telling staff about future sales. I have my own opinions on this. Telling them sooner rather than later is always going to build trust.

I advocate telling them as soon as you start planning and get them involved in the process of getting exit ready. This means you are sharing the message 3 or more years before the sale process starts and it becomes part of their internal dialogue and communication patterns. They keep it more confidential because it's just part of the daily routine and nothing to worry about.

A D-I-Y Approach

Selling your business yourself is ill-advised. If it fails, the impact can reduce your value and make your business harder to sell on better terms in the future. Especially if you end up selling your business under time pressure. If you choose this route always advertise blind (no company names etc) in the first instance to weed out the looki-loos.

The Transaction

"The worst financial transaction you will ever make is to sell yourself short."
Greg Gilbert

The Components

From the first thoughts about selling through to the final documentation is quite a journey. The exit process culminates with the signing of lots of documents, transfer of funds and handing over the keys. Here's what to expect.

Getting exit ready might feel like a hard job but it's just the "getting started" stage of the whole exit process. Let's call it phase 1. Phase 2 is the decision to sell or transfer ownership, which includes getting your Information Memorandum together and finding some eager buyers who are willing and able to acquire your business for terms that are acceptable to you.

These 2 phases are infinitely easier than the final phase, though it won't feel like it at the time. The real hard work is in getting the deal across the line and completed.

There are lots of free resources to guide you through a typical deal structure if you know what to Google. One of the best resources I found in plain language is the Midexo Guide to Due Diligence, which clearly outlines their approach, illustrated in the figure below:

Heads of Terms

Ideally you want to have several indicative offers to choose from. These need to be carefully qualified and filtered. Having a choice is a great position to be in because you can start with the one that offers you the best terms for you and potentially put any others that are attractive on ice for a short period.

Heads of Terms (HoT) sets out the commercial terms on which the deal proceeds. Though not legally binding (in most cases), it outlines terms not just the price. It includes some expected conditions that the buyer has identified as critical to a successful acquisition for them. The document usually crystalises after a bit of to and fro between buyer and seller. It isn't just a declaration from the buyer, it's the culmination of initial negotiations.

The main purpose of the HoT is:

- Written confirmation, in principle, of the main terms agreed
- An outline of the timetable
- Clarity of the obligations of both parties during the negotiations
- A guiding framework for the final legally binding contract

Before settling on the HoT, it's the opportunity to ask lots of questions and not make any assumptions. As always if in doubt, clarify. It's a lot harder, though not impossible, to clear up misunderstandings later in the process. It's always more expensive later in the process.

The HoT typically include:

- Purchase price, timing and methods of payment
- Performance criteria for final payment / price
- What's included and what's excluded in the deal

- Who is responsible for costs, including any legal requirements such as lease transfers and contract assignments?

- Post completion restrictions on the seller

- Timetable for the transaction (you don't want a DD to be endless)

- Period of exclusivity

- Confidentiality, during the process and if the deal isn't completed

Once a HoT is agreed, there is a period of exclusivity where other offers are held at bay while the due diligence period starts. Whilst, on the whole, not legally binding, certain clauses have legal force, such as confidentiality and relating to who pays costs of the subsequent elements of the transaction. The HoT is the agreed principles and intentions of both parties.

Due Diligence

The exit planning path is fraught with twists and turns and becomes extremely perilous when the due diligence (DD) process starts.

Due diligence is a forensic analysis of your business that starts with a number of checklists consisting of over 200 questions (sometimes extending into thousands). The questions look at the intricate details of every facet of your business. At some point in the process, you are guaranteed to get to the point where you ask, "How much more do they want to know?" and "When's this going to stop?" It's excruciating and stressful.

Being in good shape makes due diligence easier

Value is attributed to more than just the numbers in your business and the DD process identifies any weaknesses or risks that the buyer finds unpalatable. Knowing what the buyer is going to find BEFORE starting the process gives you a head start. It allows you to either fix things or be open about them rather than appearing defensive. Finding inherent weaknesses in your business allows the buyer to reconsider the offer price or build post-acquisition claw backs into the Sale and Purchase (SPA) Agreement.

One of the biggest success factors in the completion of an acquisition deal is seller preparation for a robust due diligence process. The more challenging the DD process is for the buyer;

the more risk they apply to the investment and the lower value they place on it. It's the reason they walk away before wasting more money on the process.

Due diligence is costly in terms of time, energy and money for both parties. Being unprepared as a seller leads to very high levels of anxiety and stress. Preparation and understanding of your business gives you a return on the investment of time and effort you have put in.

DD questions start off structured in the form of checklists. The checklists separate into a number of categories, depending on the needs of the buyer and the industry sector including:

- Financial

- Legal and contracts

- IT

- People / HR

- Tax / compliance

- Operations

- Environmental compliance

DD leaves nowhere to hide; it allows a buyer to pick apart the business, so they understand exactly what it is they are acquiring and how much effort they are going to have to put in to integrate it with their existing portfolio of investments and businesses.

What they uncover exposes elements of risk that they are unhappy with, and which are then used as an opportunity to reduce the offer price, request withholding amounts or even withdraw their offer.

Every due diligence process demands production of a comprehensive package of documentary evidence. All of the documents are gathered into a data room which is accessed by the buyer under the supervision of the sellers' lawyers and corporate brokers.

Tracking all the documents, questions and answers becomes complicated very quickly. In pre-technology days the data room was a physical library of documents and paperwork, in hundreds of files. These days there are tracking tools and electronic repositories to make life easier. It still needs methodical and diligent management.

Getting through due diligence without a professional and experienced team is, at best, a challenge if not virtually impossible. Your preparation is essential to a speedy conclusion. The longer the DD takes the more stressful it is for both sides and the more likely the sale fails to complete. Preparation for a sale reduces the stress and frustration of the DD experience.

DD is where many deals collapse for any number of reasons. Sellers get tired of the endless questions that seem to add more questions with every answer. Buyers get frustrated with the lack of accurate information or changes in the answers. Buyers discover criteria or characteristics that don't fit their acquisition profile etc.

The aim of DD is to evaluate the risks in the business. Accuracy and consistency of information about the target company gives a buyer comfort and reduces their perception of risks. It's not just a paperwork and document gathering exercise. At some point the buyer is going to want to see the business and its people in real life. They want to experience the intangible aspects of the business such as its culture.

Increases in the perception of risk can require longer earn-outs or ties-in or a financial retention as part of the final contract.

If you, as the business owner, are conducting the DD process without the support of your staff then be prepared to scan, copy, and search for what feels like a million documents. I've personally felt more attached to the photocopier and scanner during the DD process than any other item, including my bed. Being prepared really pays dividends.

In the most prepared companies, keeping an up-to-date document library saves thousands during the sale process and costs 10-15 minutes a week in normal operations.

Any worries or concerns the buyer has in DD are translated into warranties and indemnities in the SPA. It is critical for the buyer to make sure that they understand the business and basis on which the purchase is being made. Any misunderstanding can have a disastrous impact after completion. Similarly, the seller wants to reduce any post-acquisition penalties. Lawyers earn their fees at this point, on both sides.

At the risk of repeating myself, preparation is king.

Specific interest is usually taken over:

- Property and leases

- Contracts

- Employees, especially terms and conditions

- Intellectual property

- Governance and compliance

- Outstanding litigation (or potential exposure to future litigation)

The final negotiations

Once everyone has signed off the DD, it's down to the final hurdle, the actual contract for the sale of the business – the Share and Purchase Agreement. It's the final fence in the race, but, like the Grand National, you can still fall here, and if it does, your race is over (for now).

The Sale and Purchase Agreement (SPA) details every aspect of the transfer of ownership in the body and appendices. The DD outcomes decide a considerable amount of the detail for the SPA. Anything that the buyer sees as a risk becomes part of the warranties or indemnities clauses.

It must be remembered that the SPA is a joint contract between the parties who are selling and buying. It's comprehensive. It's the final step of selling a business.

Payment Terms

While the Purchase price might be set, the actual payment terms are generally more complicated. There are many ways for the terms to be applied. This includes deferring part of the payment conditional on performance criteria. This is a way of sharing the risks associated with the initial transfer and post-acquisition activity. It's a 2-way agreement so make sure you have all the protection in place, you need to know what needs to happen for you to get paid and you make sure you are in control of those activities.

This is especially important for an earn-out where you are required to work after the transfer of ownership under the new owners. It's easy to underestimate how soul destroying it can be to work for new owners when you've been the owner and controller yourself. If you sell to the kind of buyer that's going to make this difficult (or impossible) you are going to have to be prepared to walk away from the earn-out element. This is a reasonably common occurrence. With the right buyer who is culturally aligned, it can be a huge success. It's usually binary.

It's important to understand the tax implications of the payment terms to make sure you are not agreeing to something with a significant personal tax implication just because it's beneficial to the buyers. The SPA is a mutually agreed arrangement for the transfer of ownership and is likely to involve some give and take on different clauses. It's never completely one sided or straight forward.

If your buyer is a bigger company, part of the deal may be a swap of money for shares in the acquirer. It's important to understand how much the shares are worth to you and what restrictions you have on selling them. If they are listed (i.e., publicly traded) this is easier to account for as you'll have a free market on which to trade. There are usually strict timing restrictions on selling those shares.

However, if it's a minority interest in a private company you'll need to mitigate the risks with an effective shareholder agreement and clarity on how you can exit your value. It's your job to figure out what you want and get that included in the legal paperwork BEFORE you sign anything.

Shareholder agreements are one of the critical documents every business owner should have – no matter what the circumstances.

What's included?

Most businesses have working capital and cash held within them that form part of the distributable reserves of the business. They are due to the shareholders immediately before the transfer of assets. This is often forgotten about by less experienced or sophisticated sellers.

Make sure your lawyer deals with how the cash and working capital is managed in the SPA. Get tax advice on the treatment of this too. You don't want to end up with an unexpected tax bill because of the different treatments of the proceeds of the sale. Even sophisticated buyers get caught out by this. The more specific the SPA is on the treatment of cash and working capital the easier it is to close the numbers in the final deal.

It might seem obvious to get tax advice in advance of the sale process, but it helps you structure the deal and give the appropriate instructions for negotiations to your lawyer. Making part of the proceeds a contribution to your pension, for example, is a great way of making the most of some of your tax allowances.

Additionally, when you reinvest proceeds from a business sale there is currently an opportunity to defer tax liabilities and payments. And at the time of writing Entrepreneurs Relief is still available.

Earn-out clauses and employment restrictions are amongst other major elements of the SPA that affect you after the sale. It's the job of your lawyer to take you through every aspect of the document, but it is up to you to make sure you are aware of every word in the document, and its impact on you. It's a big document and can stretch to hundreds of pages.

It's the details that cause the last 5% of the deal to become the most demanding and complicated. The process to this point is tiring and stressful so it's hard to think straight when all you want to do is get it over. What appears to be a small issue missed here could cost you thousands, if not millions.

Popping the champagne corks

Nothing beats the feeling of signing that SPA and watching the funds arrive in your bank account.

But don't expect to arrive at your lawyer's office at 11am on the day of the signing and expect to be having a champagne afternoon tea. Even when all you have to do is sign a document, it's rarely that simple. Most sellers and buyers experience last minute tweaks and adjustments.

It's not unusual to still be in the lawyer's office hours later than expected or, indeed, days or weeks later.

In one exit process a client was expected to complete the deal on 30th June. Over the next 3 months there were 4 completion dates set that simply failed to complete. With one thing and another it was late September by the time the ink was drying on the SPA. By this time the sellers were completely fed up and, had one of them not been staying in the company, there would have been significant commercial damage to the business.

Despite several extensions to the deadlines for signing the final SPA, the working capital and cash agreement that was written in the SPA did not match what had been verbally agreed. This caused the seller to get a third-party auditor to independently review the final numbers (there was a deferred payment element of the deal that required specific future performance). The audit cost 5-figures but resulted in a 6-figure release of cash in favour of the seller, much to the annoyance of the buyer. It was the buyer who dropped the ball on the SPA.

In my very first exit experience the final phase of the deal was a long and complex affair involving nearly 100 people and a 700-page SPA. The company being sold included entities in different time zones which needed to be legally concluded in chunks. Starting on day one in the early hours, it finally concluded the following morning.

As the summer sun rose on the horizon of the marathon process, the lawyers, buyers and sellers emerged from an office to drink a glass of champagne and wait for the funds to come into the seller's bank accounts in multiple transfers of tens of millions in payment.

The rest of the morning was spent packing up paperwork and everyone getting ready to go home. As part of the seller team, I enjoyed an open-air post-deal lunch. It was a boisterous affair as each tranche of money arrived. When only one more transfer was left, I fell asleep, face first, in my lobster salad – only waking as the final beep of my email came through notifying me of the last payment. Having cleaned up the Rose Marie sauce from my face and hair (I still can't smell it without thinking of that day) I slept, deeply, for more than 17 hours, thankfully in my own bed.

PART 3

Getting Started

"The way to get started is to quit talking and get doing."
Walt Disney

Finding the Advisors

Your selling dream team consists of lawyers, brokers, accountants and tax advisors.

With the right preparation it also includes financial planners, wealth advisors and every other expert and specialist it takes to get you, your team and your business in the best shape to get exit ready. This team unlocks all the wealth you have invested in your business. You need to know, like and trust them to ensure you maximise your return of the sale of your business. They need to get to know you and your business to be able to help you get what you want and act in your best interest.

Lawyers

Selling a business is the final part of a long hard journey. It is a complex and emotional process. You aren't legally required to have a solicitor, but it is highly recommended that you seek professional advice from an M&A specialist rather than a high street generalist.

A bit like you'd never go to a GP for heart surgery, you want someone on your side who has been round the block a few times and knows what they are dealing with.

The lawyer drafts the sale agreement and helps you negotiate the final settlement, often hand in hand with a broker. They also help with formalising contracts held with your stakeholders i.e., customers, suppliers, and employees. Discussing your plans with your lawyer before you begin the sales process means you'll be more prepared for what is to come. This saves you a lot of stress, time, and money later on in the process.

Fees are significant in the sale process. Sellers are often surprised by this. The price you pay if you do not get the right advice is much higher if it goes wrong. Your lawyer guides you through the individual clauses in the contract paperwork. They make sure you understand the risks you are taking, your exposure to future liability and how to protect yourself. Last minute changes always arise so having a lawyer that is used to this and knows how to handle it is worth the fees. It is always your own responsibility to understand the documents you sign.

Lawyers make sure the entire process and documentation is valid. This includes any regulatory controls if they apply. When selling a business, the lawyer works as part of a team of other professionals. They can negotiate with the buyer or their lawyer if required. If you don't have a broker involved, getting a third party to negotiate is a good idea. Make sure whoever it is has the negotiation skills and knows what you want.

Brokers / M&A Advisors

M&A advisers ensure the management team are not distracted and can continue to run the business. They typically service the needs of mid-market businesses over £5m valuations.

A broker is the business equivalent of an estate agent and generally works with businesses of lower valuations. This is just a rule of thumb. It's not an absolute science. As with all professional services, there are good and not so good.

Getting the best deal for you means looking at more than one offer and making sure you ask the right questions.

It's easy to get taken in with tales of how many businesses a broker has sold. It's a better question to ask, "How many businesses have you tried to sell and what % were successful?"

"Planning is bringing the future to the present so you can do something about it now."
Alan Lakein

151

Any broker who has a low sale completion success rate is earning their fees from the process not the success. Be warned, volume brokers charge 5 -6 figure sums BEFORE they've sold your business then add on several % points for the success too.

Reputable brokers are clear on the chances of success and won't take you on if they don't think they can achieve a successful sale. Volume players won't care and will take the fees regardless of the chances of success.

A specialist in your industry sector has better chances of completing a sale and getting the highest price for your business. They can identify potential strategic acquirers willing and able to pay a higher price for the business. This includes overseas buyers which are currently acquiring UK businesses faster and for higher prices than domestic buyers.

M&A advisors act in much the same way as reputable estate agents and are often specialists in specific industries or business models. Reputable advisors let you know what buyers are looking for and how to equip yourself and your business to attract the best deals. At the very least they guide you through the process before you get started and let you know what to expect and how they work.

The best ones have an existing network of contacts that help you identify the right kind of potential buyers. Sometimes the corporate advisor does not have expertise in finding a buyer and works with a broker to find one. Both work in your interest.

Business broker / M&A advisor fees in the UK range from 1% to 10% of the sale value, in addition to legal fees and other advisory fees. As this is one of the biggest parts of the cost of selling your business it's worth spending time getting one you can work with.

Always ask:

- What industry experience does the firm have?
- Who, specifically, will be working on my sale?
- How many other deals will be going on at the same time? (How important am I to you?)
- What's the process?

- How will your firm find my buyer?

- Who do you think will be a good buyer?

- What's my business value?

- How do you ensure my confidentiality is protected?

- What documents are used – and can I see samples?

- What is your fee structure?

- How do you support me before, during and after the sale process?

Timing – again!

In the same way it's never wrong to be prepared, it's never too early to get the team in place and get started. Ideally getting started in the preparation starts 2-3 years in advance.

Exit and succession planning takes time and identifying the team of advisors during this period means you are making informed decisions based on the experience of the relationship.

Your advisor team gets to know the business and gives you advice on what adds value. This makes you more attractive to the buyers they are mixing with on a daily basis. Sometime the perfect buyer comes across the horizon while you are in preparation mode. If the timing is right and you are doing the right things to get ready, you can end up selling a bit earlier but still getting the same value.

The steps for selling a business are straightforward but not necessarily easy. Knowing how to increase the value of a business is more complicated and takes much longer.

Start with Strategic Planning

If strategic planning is one of the critical factors in business success – why doesn't everyone do it? In the sale process you must present cohesive numbers in your Information Memorandum, including objective forecasts.

Successful entrepreneurs consistently state that planning, setting goals and sharing them is a critical element of team building and getting their fledgling businesses scaled up and more profitable.

The problem is STRATEGIC PLANNING appears to be difficult, time consuming and overwhelming for many business owners.

Some of the reasons for lack of planning include:

- Feeling overwhelmed

- Lack of skill

- Don't know where to start

- Thinking it won't make a difference

- Not enough time

- It's too expensive

- I'm not looking for investment

In reality, making a plan, writing it down and measuring your progress against it is one of the biggest factors in the success of both commercial enterprises and life!   It doesn't have to be complex. In fact, the simpler the better. It should be shareable, understandable, and engaging for all the appropriate people involved in the business.

97% of business owners have no exit plan.

When you are considering selling your business, it's a good time to start delegating some of the decision making and your daily tasks. This frees you up to make progress in the exit planning. You'll be less stressed and distracted when you have a plan with priorities and clear actions. You'll feel like you are in control rather than running around in circles and getting nowhere.

The plan itself should be easy to understand with some over-arching goals at its core. Making a plan does not have to be complex. The simpler it is, the easier it is to follow and explain to others. It helps if you have a clear idea of what it is you want to achieve and, more importantly, WHY you want to achieve it.

Selling a business is not for the faint hearted!

Reminding yourself of the reasons you are doing it becomes key to keeping positive when the going gets tough. Prioritising those activities is a fundamental part of your success so make sure you get the best value for your business.

You need to take care of yourself and remember that if it were easy everyone would be doing it! Equally it is not the place for martyrs and if you don't have a passion and commitment to the sale then it might be time to reassess whether you should continue.

The difference planning makes

Failing to plan is planning to fail. A carefully, well thought out plan makes a significant difference to what you achieve in a specific period of time. Exit planning helps you and your team make the right short-term decisions to achieve long term goals. If goals are clearly articulated and joined up with a vision and shared values, then the company has a framework for making effective and speedy decisions.

Even if you aren't thinking of an exit in the immediate future, it is good to remember that nearly 60% of all business owners leave their business in unplanned circumstances. Being prepared means that no matter what happens, your biggest asset is protected.

Strategy is simply a plan of action designed to achieve a long-term or major aim. Exit planning is always strategic.

As the old saying goes "what gets measured gets managed" – or in some quotes replace "gets managed" with "gets done". A key part of the exit planning process is making progress with the appropriate actions.

Goals make it easier for activities to be prioritised. Work is focused on those activities that are important to the achievement of the long-term ambitions of the organisation. When big goals are broken down into smaller, more manageable ones they are less daunting. When goals are shared with the entire team or external partners the resulting actions reduce waste and errors.

With a plan in place, it is easier to make short term changes in direction whilst still maintaining the focus on the long-term mission. The world is changing at an increasing rate – technology developments, changes in social attitudes and legislation all impact your business and demand rapid changes in the way you operate or the way your customers perceive you.

Being flexible allows changes to be acted on more quickly in light of a lot of change. It also means if you are approached by a buyer, you can make decisions that are good for you and your business not just react to someone else's agenda.

When long-term and short-term goals are written down and shared as part of the planning activity, you are setting a framework for your team to make effective decisions without constantly referring back to you alone.

More effective, better quality decisions are made in a timely manner. It is easier to respond to any diversion from plans or prepare for contingencies if there is a plan in place. This reduces reliance on you as the owner – and increases the value of your business at the same time.

Sharing a common goal with your team increases their engagement and commitment to completing tasks that benefit the company. Having employees work toward a common goal promotes an interdependency among co-workers. If each team member pulls together, they become more productive than the sum of their parts.

A cohesive workforce increases employee satisfaction and motivation. Incentivised and collaborating employees come into work willing and prepared to deliver value. A lack of cohesion leads to a stressed and tense cohort – leading to employees who do not work well together, reducing productivity and quality.

Many business owners try and keep the exit plans a secret from their staff, but this is often ill advised. If you are in your 60s, or older, the staff may already be wondering when you are going to retire and what's going to happen to them when you do. Getting them involved engages them more and builds trust and a feeling of security.

Using a plan to measure results gives management information more context. Getting the correct measures and controls in place aides accurate and timely decision making and business growth. A history of management accounts and clearly presented management information shows buyers that the business is being run professionally and has a rational decision-making process.

Planning is often more difficult if you are starting with a blank piece of paper! Equally using someone else's complicated framework or template leads you to a plan you don't understand or that doesn't have the information you need.

Plans are only used if they are understood, and they are more easily understood if they are simple.

Regular updates and measurement of activity against targets keeps you on track. Having a time scale for the milestones makes being accountable easier. In short you can see what success looks like and the actions required to achieve each part of the plan – whilst addressing the key area of your business such as Sales, Marketing, Operations, Finance and Talent.

"If you can't explain it to a 6-year-old, you don't understand it yourself."
Albert Einstein

Know Your Business

"Your value will not be what you know; it will be what you share."
Ginni Rometty

Valuation

"98% of small business owners don't know what their business is worth" according to IBIS World. With a significant number of business owners admitting their retirement wealth is tied up in their business, this is a shocking statistic.

Most retirement planning is undertaken over many years, so it is logical to plan the extraction of your retirement wealth from your business. Knowing how much your business is worth throughout its life cycle is a good measure not only of your retirement funds but also of the business performance beyond profitability.

Add in the statistic that over 50% of all business owners leave their business through events that are unexpected and unplanned, such as death, disease, and disability, and you have another good reason to know your value.

There are four myths most common as to why a business owner hasn't had their business valued:

- It's expensive

- It takes too much time

- It's complicated

- There's no need for me to have one

Most business owners only get a formal valuation when they absolutely have to. Often this is when they are under pressure from other, unplanned events such as divorce, exit or in need of funding. Yet the truth is that a valuation is a useful exercise to undertake on a regular basis.

A business valuation can help ensure you are on track to meet your personal and business goals.

For most small and medium size companies, it's the business owner's largest financial asset, yet without knowing its value, they have no idea of their overall net worth. Are you measuring your income and dividends and making up a business value in your head? How realistic is that number?

To debunk some myths about valuation:

- It doesn't have to be expensive, typically less than £10,000 (depending on the size and complexity of the business).

- It's quick, especially if you have good financial governance and produce your annual accounts promptly.

- It's simple because a valuation is based on information you already have to produce as a company.

An indicative valuation and appraisal of your financial numbers gives you insight into your overall performance – and in some cases can benchmark you against others in your industry.

If something were to happen to you, do you have protection for your income or have your mortgage payments covered? Do you have enough, if any, protection relating to your businesses' full worth? If the worst happens, and we know this does more often than not, will you leave your family exposed to the financial impact? Especially when they are at their least able to respond. A business valuation is helpful when risk assessing the financial needs of your family should you be unable to continue to run your business.

Avoiding valuing the business is effectively sticking your head in the sand rather than facing the reality of your future wealth. There are two magic numbers you need to be able to make effective decisions on your business:

1. How much do I need for my retirement?

2. What does my business give me for funding it?

Regularly valuing your business means avoiding unpleasant surprises in the future. Knowledge leads to better decision making when planning for the future of your business, such as when to sell or even if to sell.

A valuation report also helps you gain a deeper insight into how your business is positioned and performing, helping you identify and prioritise ways to improve your business.

Benchmarking

How good is your business really? As a business owner you want to think you are the best in your industry – but how do you know whether you compare favourably with other businesses? And does it matter?

Anyone looking to buy your business compares you to the industry leaders and best practice – so it's worth knowing what they are going to find out about you. When was the last time you actually benchmarked your business? Or even looked at comparisons within different areas of your business? It's all benchmarking.

Is your business excelling and you are not aware? Or struggling and needs some extra guidance to realise that there's more ways out there to do better? The objective of benchmarking is to understand and evaluate the current position of your organisation in relation to best practice and to identify areas and means of performance improvement.

Benchmarking against best practices is a great way of testing your assumptions and developing better practices within your business.

"An investment in knowledge pays the best interest."
Benjamin Franklin

Using experience, you can objectively look at activities that led to successful outcomes and what needs to happen to replicate this in the future.

Benchmarking involves four key steps:

1.   Understand what's happening NOW in your business.

2.   Analyse what others are doing (or not doing).

3.   Compare your "now" with the analysis.

4.   Take action to close the performance gap.

Benchmarking should not be a one-off exercise. It's an ongoing improvement process to allow your business to keep developing and testing what's best practice. Benchmarks are great, but they're only useful if they are:

-   Accurate

-   Relevant

-   Followed with appropriate actions

For example, if you looked at average customer order value between industry sectors, you'd see that for eCommerce beauty stores, in 2018, it was $70.71. It's not going to compare favourably to the average order value in travel ($375.05) for example – but that doesn't mean it's bad. If the benchmark isn't relevant to you or your business, then it's not helpful in any way. Knowing what's relevant is key.

Benchmarking is an opportunity to identify strengths. It's also a chance to critically appraise areas for improvement. Testing your assumptions means you ask, "is there a better way?"

Just seeing what other businesses are doing opens your business to new ideas – new ways of doing things, what to stop doing and what to start. As with all knowledge, the real power is in the action taken.

Understanding of the value of knowing benchmarks

Benchmarking has the potential to be a powerful tool in the development of a culture of continuous improvements in your business. If you rely on only internal measures, you risk limiting your perspective. High performing companies strive to identify and improve processes, product and services that are important to their customers.

Evaluating your efficiency and effectiveness against others who lead your industry or who innovate in other sectors leads to a step change in performance.

There are many different types of benchmarking:

- **Strategic:** looks at core competencies, developing new products and services, and changes in the external environment. This is long-term thinking and actions may be difficult to implement. The focus is re-aligning business strategies that have become inappropriate or irrelevant.

- **Performance or Competitive:** utilises data analysis through trade associations or third parties to protect confidentiality. This allows you to assess performance in key areas or activities in comparison with others and finding ways of closing gaps in performance.

- **Process Benchmarking:** focusing on processes and operations by seeking out best practice organisations that perform similar work or deliver similar services helps identify improvements in key processes to obtain quick benefits.

- **Functional Benchmarking:** where there are no specific or easy comparisons, looking at business sectors and areas of activity is a great way of improving similar functions or work processes, leading to innovation and significant improvements.

- **Internal Benchmarking:** assessing operations from within the same organisation, for example business units in different locations or countries can lead to quicker and easier implementation. Many a team or business has got to the top by using 1% increases in performance.

- **External Benchmarking:** is analysis of outside organisations that are known to be the best in class. Learning from those who lead the field is an opportunity to reflect and move the business forward. It takes time and resources. The credibility of the findings relies on having comparable data and appropriate information. It's a good way to develop an action plan.

It's important to take care of who you compare yourselves to. A big company may be aspirational in terms of turnover, but they may very well be inefficient as a result of their size. Critical analysis is key.

How to find out where you sit in your industry

Are you drinking your own Kool-Aid? If you are preoccupied with your own business, you easily lose sight of competitors and innovations across your industry. Keeping a finger on the pulse of the changing demands of customers means you are more prepared for change in general and maybe positively ahead of the curve.

Looking outside your own industry for the best-in-class performance of specific processes, services or approaches challenges your assumptions and tests your business practices.

For example, Southwest Airlines famously analysed Formula 1 racing pit crews to improve their airplane turn-around time at the gate. The outcome? Southwest reconfigured its gate maintenance, cleaning, and customer loading operations, and has saved the company millions of dollars per year. This made it consistently profitable when most airlines were barely breaking even.

Improving your customer service, for example, may result from comparison of processes and key performance indicators of successful competitors or shining lights in other industries. By identifying differences, you can start improving processes to strengthen your performance.

For example, Pal's Sudden Service is a small hamburger and hot dog chain and is so successful at achieving best-in-class performance for drive-thru and overall restaurant operations, that it has opened an educational institute to train other organizations. Many companies in the fast-food market use Pal's as a best-in-class benchmark for their own operations.

McDonald's has its own university for serving and business management - and according to the press, it's harder to get into than Oxford or Cambridge! (Source: *The Daily Mirror*; 25th October 2015).

Note: Trade associations often publish comparative data invaluable to the benchmarking process.

How investors look at your business

Any investor or potential buyer compares your business to others – they look for opportunities to add value. Do you have great practices in your business that they can apply to other businesses they are invested in?

A buyer wants to understand how you are positioned in the market to assess your relative value. Benchmarking uses financial or numeric data because it's most commonly available. Use of statistics such as the number of employees, floor space utilised, total equipment or assets help to understanding your business efficiency. Many of these measures of efficiency don't stand out from your management accounts.

Non-Financial Risks

The value of your business is more than just the numbers. It also considers the way your business operates.

Whilst PROFIT is an important part of the value of a business, it is only one of a multitude of factors that buyers consider when acquiring a company. Putting yourself into the buyer's shoes is a good start. This allows you to understand the areas of your business that add a genuine, material return on investment.

Anyone looking at your business wants clarity and comfort for what they're investing in, lending to, or buying. Thinking like a buyer means you know what activity maximises the value of the business. This makes you and the business prepared to achieve a successful exit. Giving priority to the issues that are extreme or urgent and resolving them quickly means you are reducing the risks. You are protecting the value of your business.

Actions = VALUE

Implementation takes time and effort. It is why most business owners don't take the necessary actions. After all, if it was easy everyone would be doing it. Not acting diminishes the value of their business as a result.

But where do you start?

Identifying which levers to pull to change the value of the business results in increased value if those levers are actually pulled. When action is taken, it's not unusual to see the value of the business increased by 20%, 30% and even 40% or 50%.

The non-financial KPIs look at 5 key areas of the business:

- Governance

- Strategy and planning

- People

- Financial management and reporting

- Risk management

It is improvement in these areas that positively impact the "multiple" and make for a much more attractive investment for buyers. Changing the performance of the non-financials invariably leads to improved profitability as a by-product.

This means work here is a win-win.

Some non-financial questions you need to answer are:

1. Are you legally up to date with HMRC and other requirements?

2. Do you have a strategic plan that's documented and acted upon?

3. Do your people have the right skills and roles (and paid accordingly)?

4. Have you got the right financial reporting in place to make decisions?

5. How do you address risk management, such as business continuity plans and insurance?

Acquirers look at what you've done as an owner to address these issues. Anything that's missing makes a buyer look in more depth at your business and put you on the back foot during the sale process. These factors ADD VALUE!

Making sure you are legally up to date AND do not have a trail of past misdemeanours shows a buyer that you've been running a professional company and reduces the worry factor when the due diligence process starts.

Having a strategic plan that everyone can understand and buy into brings your team together. It allows everyone to see the long-term goals and work towards them. This leads to more teamwork, better efficiency, and a happier place to work. A strategic plan removes uncertainty and gives clarity on the targets and direction the company is going in.

People make better decisions faster when they have a road map.

Having a strategic plan also allows for reduced reliance on the business owner. This one action alone adds huge value to the business. Side benefits are usually reduced business owner stress, great team coherence and improved efficiency and performance. Happy staff lead to happy customers, leading to greater profitability and easier customer retention.

Strategic Planning Session anyone?

Exit readiness

How easy would it be for you to just handover the keys to your business and walk away with your proceeds?

Exit readiness is about how dependant the business is on the owner. There are other factors such as financial and corporate governance, product / intellectual property, and the business model.

Separating the 3 roles that a business owner takes on is essential for getting exit ready. The 3 roles are Shareholder, Director and Employee. When these roles are blended and bundled together it's difficult for anyone to know which role the business owner is performing at any one time.

Here's a quick summary:

- Shareholder – you OWN the business, you don't control the day to day, you set the strategic direction and the expectation of the return on your capital. There are very separate liabilities, responsibilities, rights, and duties.

- Directors – you CONTROL the business, implementing the strategy to give the shareholders their return while also looking after all the stakeholders such as employees, creditors, and legal requirements (health and safety, compliance etc). There are extensive legal liabilities, responsibilities, and duties.

- Employees – a fair day's pay for a fair day's work. Most business owners are in a job. It's essential to recognise this job role also has responsibilities and should be treated as any other employee is in this role.

Get clear on role separation BEFORE thinking about selling and you will save thousands and a lot of time.

"Begin with the end in mind."
Stephen Covey

Credit worthiness

Many acquirers look to finance the purchase of your business in some way. YOUR BUSINESS' creditworthiness has an impact on their ability to raise finance.

If you are raising finance, your creditworthiness influences how much it costs you in interest.

The balance of debt in your business compared to the share capital and reserves is a key measure used in banking assessments of credit worthiness, especially when seeking additional or extensions of existing debt facilities. How easily can your business repay the loan capital and interest from available cash flow? How long does it take to pay the debt back? And what happens to the debt if you were to close the business? These are all questions that anyone looking at your business wants to be able to answer with certainty.

Action Plan

"Words may inspire but only action creates change."
Simon Sinek

What Gets Measured....

If you understand how your business is valued, you can start to measure these metrics and build long term, capital value as well as your operational profits – and be able to balance the two in your decision-making.

EBITDA is commonly used as a base value that is applied to a business looking to sell. Value is EBITDA times a "multiple", which depends on your industry and business model and a number of other factors. It's a very blunt instrument to measure the economic value of your business. It is not, by any means the only method of valuing your business (note: EBITDA = Earnings Before Interest, Tax, Depreciation and Amortization).

Earnings are your net profit before you've charged the cost of borrowing. Depreciation and amortization are simply the spreading of the economic value of the purchase of fixed assets. Depreciation being implied economic cost of tangible fixed assets, such as machinery and cars in a financial year.

Amortization is the spreading of the economic value of intangible assets, for example, goodwill, intellectual property, or patents, for example. There are specific accounting rules for intangible assets which you should discuss with your accountant.

Measuring non-financial metrics is uncommon in most small and medium size businesses. I've seen multi-million turnover businesses with a very poor grip on basic financial reporting let alone anything non-financial. It doesn't have to be complicated. Nor does it have to be a full suite of real time data put in place overnight. Start with some simple metrics first and build up your business dashboards.

The more relevant the data, the more likely it is tracked, especially if it's a measure of performance that is linked to the financial rewards of your team. Deciding what to measure in your business, and why, is a challenge. If you want to brainstorm effective performance indicators, this is a good exercise to get your employees involved in.

Where to start

Once you have valued your business and diagnosed where the strengths and weaknesses in your business lay, you know where help and intervention can be quickly focused. You discover where the biggest impact can happen, not only to your business but to your life.

Big things happen when you get the little things right. You just need to know what the little things are first. A business without goals or targets rarely achieves anywhere near the success that one with a clear action plan does.

If they are in writing, then the chances of success significantly increase. It sounds complicated but as you see in the Planning chapter of this book, it can be made simpler and much quicker than you might have imagined. Simplicity is the key to getting started.

Without insight and information on how the business is performing, the effectiveness of decision-making is diminished. A business may fail, or fly based on the adequacy of the decisions made by the senior management team (even if that team is one person – you, the business owner!)

Having some basic management accounts and key performance indicators on a regular and consistent basis helps you fly your business in the right direction rather than as if you were blind. Do you already have the information? Is it regularly produced to a high standard of accuracy?

Do you need to build some reports from scratch? It does not have to be complicated. Keeping it simple is the way you keep on top of it. Many accountants produce sheets of numbers that make no sense to the leadership team in a business, which makes the whole activity an expensive waste of time.

As you start to grow and bring in new team members, having systems creates consistency which avoids compromising your standards of service delivery. Everyone knowing their role in the organisation is one of the most commonly missed parts of the system. And systems don't mean technology – apps and software are simply the tools of a system.

It's processes and procedures that are critical to a scalable business.

Having the right skills and attitudes to allow expansion of the business and liberate YOU from working **IN** the business to working **ON** it is a critical factor for scaling-up.

Many business owners do not see the value of bringing people into their organisations with the skills and attitudes that allow them to be released from some tasks to achieve more – and generally that translates into earning more.

Seeing people only as a cost is a sure-fire way of keeping your business smaller than it needs to be. Building a team is not easy and looking after staff, if you don't get the right ones on board, can be debilitating and demotivating.

Having a serious commitment to monitoring and managing cash means you will have a business where the life blood of the business, CASH, flows through it. Without a flow of cash, the business quickly seizes up.

Running out of cash is one of the most common problems in business failure. Understanding the difference between cash and profit is essential for every business owner. Getting this wrong kills your business.

Your business is not a job, though it often feels like the worst job in the world! The most successful business owners are driven by a bigger purpose than having an income that covers their survival needs. They have a passion and drive that exceeds the average employee. They take risks to achieve a bigger life and appear to be driven by wealth.

More commonly it's not wholly about money at all – it's about the things that financial freedom can buy. If you don't have the energy and conviction for your business, how can you inspire others to feel that way too? Being tired of your business or losing the passion is a key indicator that you should think about getting your business ready for your exit – either by selling or by building a management team to get you out of the day-to-day activity.

My first conversation with a new client who knew it was time to leave his business started with his declaration "I know I'm becoming the biggest problem in the business, and I know I'm holding it back". After over 2 decades of riding the entrepreneurial roller coaster he wants to explore other adventures and take the weight of his business off his shoulders.

He's ready to step out of the day to day and only work at a strategic level while he develops his senior management team. But, as long as he turns up to work every day, the team still defer to his decision making. He has to let go and allow them to fail, which is scary. It won't happen overnight but it's already taking huge leaps froward.

Reverse Due Diligence

Undertaking your own due diligence process is a great way to see your business from the perspective of a buyer AND give the process a dry run without the pressure of time and external oversight.

There are more details of the DD process in the chapters on Legals and The Transaction. If your team of advisors is in place, they will give you a basic DD checklist (in reality it's a series of checklists on different subjects).

Working your way through these is good preparation for your future, whether that's selling, passing on to the next generation or transferring to employees. You end up with a company "bible" of important documents as well as the opportunity to re-look at some of the contracts and commitments that may be well overdue for renegotiation or simply cancellation.

Being able to do this over a period of time is a lot less stressful than the mad dash to get a data room populated and up to date (the documents required for formal "seller" or vendor due diligence).

Employee Participation

I've seen business owners tie themselves in knots trying to keep everything in the business a secret from their employees. Yet transparency and clarity set you and your business free.

It all starts with recruiting personnel for values and attitudes over skills. This might sound counter intuitive – especially when you know you need a specific skillset – but getting your team full of people who share values and support each other is much easier in the long term than trying to retrain a highly skilled person in new attitudes. I'd argue that retraining values is impossible!

Having worked in an environment where one critical skill was required and the individual who had it was already in the organisation and definitely not a team player, I can testify to how destructive misalignment of values can be.

At its worst, the rest of the team exercised a targeted programme of isolation to the individual, making decisions without him and then finding ways of getting his passive buy in. The energy and distraction this took was notable and the rest of the team came to resent the challenging individual whilst grudgingly recognising how his specific skill contributed to the project. As soon as the project was complete, the individual was legally and joyfully expelled from the team – and ultimately from the company.

If you have worked in any big organization, you know exactly what I am writing about here. Shared values are critical to overall success and team dynamics. When you have the right team, you're happy to engage them in the planning process, including in exit planning. It makes the journey easier for you and them.

As the company grows and develops the skills and experience required changes over time. Some employees come in with lower levels of skill that allows them to grow and develop into new roles with the organisation. Others join with high levels of skill and eventually can't get the professional development they need within the organisation. They leave for new challenges OR stay and become dissatisfied and potentially destructive, possibly passive and disillusioned.

Understanding who you've got in your team makes planning for these circumstances easier. You can have honest conversations with employees about their contribution to the value of the business and remunerate them accordingly.

In my first exit experience I was the last one out of the business HQ which was made gradually redundant as the disposal of the business was completed over a period of 18 months. I was happy to stay until I switched off the lights and locked the office door for the last time because I'd been party to the entire plan from the beginning – it took 4 years!

Having a clear structure for delegating decision-making to the people in your organisation requires that you also invest them with appropriate levels of authority, responsibility and accountability to enable them to perform effectively. Trusting people to make the right decisions, within a framework, allows them to flourish and you to get on with strategic planning and actions.

Most people come to work to do a good job – you have to get out of the way and let them! Recognising that as a company grows, the structure of the organisation also needs to change is often missed by busy CEOs, yet it is essential to keep the organisation functioning effectively, efficiently and relevantly.

The Final Event

At some point you are going to be at your leaving party, assuming everything goes to plan. It may be that, like many business owners, you slip away without much fanfare. Have you thought what that looks and feel like?

After all the stress of preparing your business then going through a transaction process, you might have not given a lot of thought as to what happens next. When I left my first business, having sold my shares, resigned as a director and handed over the day job, I had a few weeks of just decompressing and resting. But then came the day when I realised I had no purpose. It was a very empty feeling.

Worse than that was the feeling after my first visit back to the business. Seeing it run without me and the team seemingly having not missed me for a moment left me devastated. Yet it was evidence that I'd done the right things. The business operated smoothly without me. In fact, it ran better without me getting in the way with my ownership thinking. It's a matter of pride that it's still going nearly 20 years later.

If you engage with your employees, you can enjoy a team celebration of the business transfer. They might go back to the day job the following day whereas you are on a different path, but you avoid the very hollow feeling of it just being a transaction.

"Coming together is beginning, staying together is progress, working together is success."
Henry Ford

192

What next?

"The only real problem in life is what to do next."
Arthur C. Clarke

What are you going to do now?

What you've learned in this book helps you get through a successful sale process – and be happy with the result. But only if you act.

When you have a business that is exit ready, you have a richer, happier future. But there's a problem. Most business owners only sell a business once in their lifetime and they don't know how to get ready or what the process is.

Think about how your life and your business would transform with an exit plan that adds more value. Imagine how much more cash you'll get if you knew what to work on every day that adds the most value to your business. When you have a clearly defined Exit Readiness Plan, you have more than just a business. You have a more valuable and attractive business that's easier to sell on better terms.

Working through this book you've found out why you need to get your business exit ready with an actionable Exit Readiness Plan that gives you the focus and direction for your business exit.

You can now create the Exit Readiness Plan that's right for you to get more from your life, your team, and your business.

Your Exit Readiness Plan will:

- Create a clear and prioritised implementation plan

- Show how to increase the VALUE of your business

- Increase productivity

- Help you recruit better talent

- Help make your business easier to sell for better terms

Stop guessing the value of your business. Instead, know that your business is moving towards greater value so you can have a richer, happier future.

"You only live once, but if you do it right, once is enough."
Mae West

The checklists

Building an Exit Readiness Plan is relatively simple but isn't necessarily easy. You have so many options sometimes it can be difficult to choose.

The hardest part is getting started. Here's some simple checklists to get you heading in the right direction.

Each list is a self-contained project and can be used in any order depending on where your business is.

Business Basics Assessment		
1	Do you have a strategic plan for your business?	
2	Do you have management information for decision making?	
3	Do your systems support customers getting excellent service?	
4	Do you have the right people in your business to achieve its full potential?	
5	Do you have monthly cash flow statements and forecasts?	
6	How reliant is your business on YOU?	

195

Are YOU ready to sell? It's not just about the business, it's about your own beliefs and approach. More business sales fail because the seller is just not ready than any other reason. Here's 6 essential questions:

Pre-Sale "Self" Assessment		
1	Why am I selling?	
2	Is it the right time? (for me, for the business?)	
3	Am I ready?	
4	Is the business in the best shape to sell?	
5	What's it worth?	
6	Who are the potential buyers?	

Getting the right broker or M&A advisor can be a challenge, here's some questions to ask when you are choosing. These can also be used for your lawyers too.

	M&A Advisor / Broker Selection Questions	
1	What industry experience does the firm have?	
2	Who, specifically, will be working on my sale?	
3	How many other deals will be going on at the same time? (How important am I to you?)	
4	What's the process?	
5	How will your firm find my buyer?	
6	Who do you think will be a good buyer?	
7	What's my value?	
8	How do you ensure my confidentiality is protected?	
9	What documents are used – and can I see samples?	
10	What is your fee structure?	
11	How do you support me before, during and after the sale process?	

Processes are usually written as Standard Operating Procedures and have a consistent format. They are designed to be easily understood. They teach and optimise specific activities through all the steps required to complete a particular task. In the first instance simply writing down what you currently do in a set of circumstances is the start to getting processes in place. It always must start with something.

PROCESSES – Getting Started	
1	What is the goal or desired outcome of this process?
2	When does the process begin and end?
3	What activities move the process forward?
4	What departments and/or employees are involved?
5	What information is being transferred between steps?

When you look at scalability, you ask the questions "what does the future business look like?" and "how can we scale this?". It's time to get into the detail and build the commercial model that shows how to scale revenue, costs, and the people. There is no point in developing a great product that isn't profitable or capable of being profitable when you add in the level of support required to meet customer expectations. Start thinking about:

	BUSINESS SCALABILTY ASSESSMENT	
1	What is the product / service offering to the customer?	
2	How does it get delivered?	
3	How much is it sold for and what is the support cost?	
4	Who is in the team now?	
5	What do you need in skills and experience to scale?	
6	How quickly can you scale?	
7	When do you need to start?	
8	What volumes of customer can you cope with now?	
9	At what stages of growth do you need to build up your delivery resources?	

Running a company has legal requirements in the UK and it can cause you and your business significant disruption if you don't get them sorted out – the earlier the better. Ignorance of the law is no defence and some of the requirements come with hefty penalties if not complied with, ranging from fines to imprisonment for major dereliction of duties. This is a limited list of the essentials:

	COMPANY COMPLIANCE ESSENTIALS	
1	Is the company up to date with paying taxes?	
2	Do all your employees have up-to-date and compliant Employment contracts?	
3	Do you have employment policies and procedures (Grievance, Disciplinary) - and do the employees have copies of them?	
4	Does the company have appropriate Employers Liability Insurance?	
5	Does the company have Health and Safety policy statements?	
6	Are annual reports of company shareholders up to date?	
7	Is the company compliant with Data Protection?	
8	Have annual financial statements been submitted on time?	

Whilst not required legally, the following are also useful to your business and should be considered as essential activities that make being in business easier in the long term:

	SHAREHOLDER PROTECTION ESSENTIALS	
1	A shareholder agreement (if more than one shareholder)	
2	Directors service agreements	
3	A buy / sell agreement and cross option agreement	
4	Business Insurance beyond the legal minimum i.e., key man, business interruption etc	
5	Terms and Conditions – specifically tailored for your business	
6	IP and trademark protection	

This book is not a specialist health and safety book and using the guidance on the Health and Safety Executive website is advised[1]. In the UK there are 8 main pieces of legislation (as at 2021):

HEALTH AND SAFETY LEGISLATION ESSENTIALS		
1	The Management of Health and Safety at Work Regulations 1999	
2	The Workplace (Health, Safety and Welfare) Regulations 1992	
3	The Health and Safety (Display Screen Equipment) Regulations 1992	
4	The Personal Protective Equipment at Work Regulations 1992	
5	The Manual Handling Operations Regulations 1992	
6	The Provision and Use of Work Equipment Regulations 1998	
7	The Reporting of Injuries, Diseases and Dangerous Occurrences Regulations 1995	
8	The Working Time Regulations 1998 (as amended)	

[1] http://www.hse.gov.uk/

There are too few accountants who are committed to really adding value and it is worth the hunt to find them.

Some questions to ask before engaging your first accountant or benchmarking your current accountant against

ACCOUNTANT ASSESSMENT		
1	Are they pro-active?	
2	Do they charge by the hour?	
3	How quickly do they respond?	
4	Does your accountant take your money or make you money?	
5	Do you know exactly what to expect from them?	
6	Are they really interested in me and my business?	

If your accountant is proactive and engaged in your success, they will be answering the following questions:

10 QUESTIONS YOUR ACCOUNTANT SHOULD BE ASKING YOU	
1	Are you paying too much tax? If yes, how much and why?
2	Can you get a refund of any of the tax you've overpaid?
3	Are you up to date with legal compliance? If not, how can I get up to date?
4	How are your profit levels compared to other businesses your size?
5	How's your cashflow going?
6	Talk about your business numbers - and what they mean
7	What is your business worth?
8	How do you pay yourself?
9	Are you on track to achieve your business and personal goals?
10	If your accountant isn't delivering, then your next question is: What's involved in changing accountants and moving to one who is going to give you the support and answers?

One of the things that extends the length of the sale process is a lack of seller preparation. Here's the bare minimum that you'll need to prepare for both your Information Memorandum and the Due Diligence process.

INFORMATION MEMORANDUM ESSENTIALS		
1	Three years statutory financial statements	
2	Five years of projected financials	
3	A full description of the company including history current operations, and future growth opportunities	
4	A SWOT analysis on the business	
5	An analysis of the projected growth of your industry	
6	Assessment of the markets and projected growth	
7	Overview of top clients	
8	Overview of critical suppliers	
9	List of significant contractual relationships with suppliers/customers	
10	An organisational chart, list of key employees and contractual relationships with the company	
11	Details of off-balance sheet assets (IP etc.)	

Need help?

If you want to get more from your business – and make your business worth more and need some help, then it's a great time to get a Value Assessment of your business.

Are you one of the thousands of business owners who dreams of selling your business for millions and sailing into the sunset of your retirement on the velvet cushion of wealth? If you've spent a lifetime of hard work and sacrifice building your business and you are now looking for help, then you are in the right place.

Most business owners only sell or leave their business once and have no idea what the process is before they go into a sale transaction. They often leave money on the table because they aren't prepared. That's a tragedy that's costing business owners millions.

The harsh reality is:

- 80% of businesses never get sold

- Over ½ of all business owners leave their business because of unplanned or unexpected events

- Fewer than 40% of business owners have any succession or exit plans

This means:

- The business is worth less than they hoped

- They feel stuck with no clear way out of their business

- There's a high risk the business will fade away to nothing

You can make your Business Worth More simply by:

1. Get it valued with a **Value Assessment Report**

2. Build an actionable Exit Readiness plan

3. Implement the Plan

It's time to stop rolling the dice with your business value and get what you deserve from your business. With a Value Assessment you will:

1. Make more money

2. Reduce the risk of fading away

3. Be the hero in your business

The Solution is simple – it starts with a phone call

A VALUE Assessment finds all the strengths and addresses all the weaknesses in your business that reduce its value and make it difficult to sell or transfer ownership. You can then spend the time and effort on the things that are going to make a real difference to your financial future AND give you a business that thrives and lasts long after you've moved on.

How the VALUE Assessment works in 3 simple steps:

1. The VALUE Assessment – lets you know where your business is right now and what's diminishing the value of your business.

2. Build a priority ACTION PLAN so that you know what needs to happen to add the most value for the least effort.

3. IMPLEMENTATION with support and guidance from someone who's been on the journey many times before

and can transfer the knowledge and experience to you and your team. I'm with you all the way.

Leaving you with a business that is worth more, makes more profit and can run without you when you are ready to leave. Here's what you get:

Benefits	
Business	**Shareholders**
Make more profit	Less stress
Higher value	More cash
Easier to sell	More time
Lasts longer	A more valuable asset

Designed for business owners, founders and senior leadership teams in owner managed businesses, the Value Assessment helps you build a business that is attractive to buyers, investors, and employees alike.

It also helps you:

- Decrease staff turnover

- Connect with the right customers

- Lead your team more effectively

- Increase your reputation in your industry (and business in general)

2 things every business should have in place from the start:

- A succession plan. Succession Planning means that the business is not built around a single or few key individuals. This de-risks the business, making it worth more. Investing in the RIGHT people doing the RIGHT things at the RIGHT time for the RIGHT reasons always increases profits and adds long term value.

- An exit plan means that no matter what happens, your business can operate without you and isn't at risk of fading away when you lose the capacity or energy to keep it going.

Being in business is hard enough; investing in a Value Assessment can add millions and save you thousands in the long run. It is an investment that will help your business survive and thrive.

About the author – Who am I?

I am Christine Nicholson, an author, speaker, and award-winning Professional Business Mentor who works with multi-million turnover companies with founders who still work in the day-to-day management of their technology, engineering, or product services businesses.

I am proud that my clients have made me UK Business Mentor of the Year 2020. And to be named one of the global Top 50 Women in Accounting for 2020 for my work with finance teams. I was a finalist in the National Entrepreneur Awards 2017 - and my client won the award – and I've appeared on BBC talking about business!

I have received the highest Professional Award as a Business Mentor from the Association of Business Mentors and I am a Court Assistant and Freeman of the Company of Entrepreneurs of the City of London.

I've been helping businesses for over 30 years - experiencing the successes and failures, making mistakes along the way, and discovering how to avoid them. I built my first business from £0 to £4.5m highly profitable turnover in less than 15 months. I then helped a client rescue their high-tech engineering company from bankruptcy to an 8-figure exit in 18 months. Along the way I've worked with every type of business from software companies to taking over the running of a zoo.

Walking in the founders' shoes and living to tell the tale enables me to help other business owners become the heroes in their businesses. My clients have always increased turnover, profitability, and cash – they've made millions and saved themselves thousands in the process.

Better businesses lead to a better world not just for now but for our future. Currently over 80% of businesses do not get sold, leaving business owners closing their doors on a lifetime of work - making just 1% difference to that number could have a huge positive impact on those businesses, communities, and society as a whole.

I believe there is incredible power when GREAT IDEAS meet SUCCESSFUL IMPLEMENTATION - I get excited when I can work with someone who has a great idea and successfully implements the appropriate actions.

What's it like to work with me?

You'll have the kind of regular, knowledgeable support you have been missing in your business. Even when I'm not in your business I'm at the end of the phone or email whenever you need me.

You'll quickly create a vision and build a strategic plan that includes every area of your business - not just finance but people, operations, and sales. We'll test your profit potential and look at how we can leverage it to achieve more than you thought possible.

You'll be on the path to a healthier, happier business for everyone involved. In a very short period, you'll have an actionable road map for:

- Working fewer hours,

- Less stress and anxiety,

- Your business will be worth more,

- You'll have improved profitability and

- More certainty around your cash flow.

What drives me:

I've written multiple books on running successful businesses - one of which is used by accountants to help their client understand finance:

- 5 Minute Finance – The Business Owners' Guide to Understanding Your Numbers

- What's Your Profit Score? – Your Fast Track to Business Success

- How to B.U.I.L.D a Unicorn – 5 Steps to a Successful Technology Business

All books available on Amazon - www.amazon.co.uk/s?k=Christine+nicholson&ref=nb_sb_noss

Or in print - www.3ppublishing.co.uk/authors/christine-nicholson

I've worked in many different industries and countries, and I know what works. Along my journey I've worked for two royal families, I've run a zoo, rescued a charity, and dug up the biggest

216

unexploded WW2 bomb found in the UK. All in an entrepreneur's day's work, nothing surprises me, and I am known for being a straight talking, safe pair of hands.

I wasn't born a Business Owner

After a couple of years as a junior clerk in a high street bank, I fulfilled my sense of adventure by joining the Women's Royal Naval Service (WRNS). By my mid 20s I knew I was capable of more than my limited school achievement, so I studied hard to become a Chartered Management Accountant. Later I satisfied another ambition by getting a Law degree and I have a post grad qualification in Information Systems Management.

I've seen the impact of failing businesses. I've also seen the impact successful business have on their communities and society. Entrepreneurship is all about ideas and gets a lot of coverage - but running businesses, the engine room part of a business, is the poor cousin and gets almost no glory at all. It isn't taught in schools or universities and leaves many business owners floundering when they should be thriving.

When I was a kid, I saw my favourite uncle start a business he had a real passion for and was good at, but his business ultimately failed. It was only later as an adult I really began to understand why that happened and the impact it had on him and his family. If he had had better business insight and knowledge then his business could have been thriving, employing more people, and creating wealth for all stakeholders.

I believe that business doesn't have to be complicated, but it's made that way because of a lack of knowledge, support, and available business education. I believe business should (and can) be fun and make a positive impact on the world.

References & Reading

Aldrich, P. and Pullman, A., 2019. Building an Outstanding Workforce: Developing People to Drive Individual and Organizational Success. 1st ed. UK: Kogan Page.

Anderton, P., 2021. Clarity is Power. Northants: 3P Publishing.

BHP, 2021. The BHP guide to selling your business. BHP Corporate Finance.

Deloitte, 2020. The state of the deal: M&A trends 2020. Deloitte.

Kengelbach, J., Keienburg, G., Degen, D., Sollner, T., Kashyrkin, A. and Sievers, S., 2020. The 2020 M&A Report: Alternative Deals Gain Traction. [online] BCG. Available at: <https://www.bcg.com/en-gb/publications/2020/mergers-acquisitions-report-alternative-deals-gain-traction> [Accessed 20 May 2021].

Lewis, A. and McKone, D., 2021. So Many M&A Deals Fail Because Companies Overlook This Simple Strategy. [online] Harvard Business Review - Mergers and Acquisitions. Available at: <https://hbr.org/2016/05/so-many-ma-deals-fail-because-companies-overlook-this-simple-strategy> [Accessed 20 May 2021].

McCarthy, B., 2020. Council Post: How An Ownership Mindset Can Change Your Team's Culture. [online] Forbes. Available at:

<https://www.forbes.com/sites/forbesfinancecouncil/2020/04/15/how-an-ownership-mindset-can-change-your-teams-culture/?sh=5297b7e84b8b> [Accessed 29 March 2021].

Midaxo. 2021. M&A Guide: Due Diligence. [online] Available at: <https://resources.midaxo.com/guide-due-diligence> [Accessed 17 March 2021].

Nicholson, C., 2018. What's Your Profit Score?: Your Fast Track to Bus. 1st ed. Northants: 3P Publishing.

Office for National Statistics, 2021. Mergers and acquisitions involving UK companies: October to December 2020. Statistical bulletin. Office for National Statistics.

PwC. 2021. Global M&A Industry Trends. [online] Available at: <https://www.pwc.com/gx/en/services/deals/trends.html> [Accessed 20 May 2021].

Schwantes, M., 2017. 12 Ways to Identify the Future Leaders of Your Company Right Now. [online] Inc. Available at: <https://www.inc.com/marcel-schwantes/first-90-days-how-to-identify-the-future-leaders-of-your-company-right-now.html> [Accessed 20 May 2021].